Cambridge El

Elements in Perception
edited by
James T. Enns
The University of British Columbia

CHEMICAL SENSES IN FEEDING, BELONGING, AND SURVIVING

Or, Are You Going to Eat That?

Paul A. S. Breslin
*Rutgers, The State University of New Jersey
and the Monell Chemical Senses Center*

CAMBRIDGE
UNIVERSITY PRESS

University Printing House, Cambridge CB2 8BS, United Kingdom

One Liberty Plaza, 20th Floor, New York, NY 10006, USA

477 Williamstown Road, Port Melbourne, VIC 3207, Australia

314–321, 3rd Floor, Plot 3, Splendor Forum, Jasola District Centre, New Delhi – 110025, India

79 Anson Road, #06–04/06, Singapore 079906

Cambridge University Press is part of the University of Cambridge.

It furthers the University's mission by disseminating knowledge in the pursuit of education, learning, and research at the highest international levels of excellence.

www.cambridge.org
Information on this title: www.cambridge.org/9781108714075
DOI: 10.1017/9781108644372

First published 2019

A catalogue record for this publication is available from the British Library.

ISBN 978-1-108-71407-5 Paperback
ISSN 2515-0502 (online)
ISSN 2515-0499 (print)

Chemical Senses in Feeding, Belonging, and Surviving

Or, Are You Going to Eat That?

Elements in Perception

DOI: 10.1017/9781108644372
First published online: July 2019

Paul A. S. Breslin
Rutgers, The State University of New Jersey and The Monell Chemical Senses Center

Author for correspondence: breslin@monell.org

Abstract: This Element looks at the physiological and social roles of taste and the proximal chemical senses. First, how we perceive food and people when we contact them is discussed. These perceptions help us identify what we are eating and with whom we are present and serves as an analysis of the complex scene. Second, the influence of taste in food choice, metabolism, and nutrition is considered. Next, the impact of taste and the proximal chemical senses in social interactions is examined, including social eating. Then, the role of taste and the proximal chemical senses in emotion is explored.

Keywords: taste, smell, feeding, sex, emotion

ISBNs: 9781108714075 (PB), 9781108644372 (OC)
ISSNs: 2515-0502 (online), ISSN 2515-0499 (print)

Contents

1 Introduction

In this Element, I discuss the physiological and social roles of taste and the proximal chemical senses. First, I discuss from a chemosensory perspective how we perceive food and people when we contact them. These perceptions help us identify what we are eating and with whom we are present and serves as an analysis of the complex scene. Second, I consider the influence of taste in food choice, metabolism, and nutrition. Next, the impact of taste and the proximal chemical senses in social interactions is considered, including social eating. Then, I discuss the role of taste and the proximal chemical senses in emotion, which includes the emotions related to feeding and social interactions. Throughout, I propose and illustrate the influence of the proximal chemical senses in the rich interconnections of all of these ideas; a set of experiences, emotions, and perceptions that influence each other fluidly. The continuous interplay of sensation, perception, feeding, social gathering, bonding, sex, and emotions place the proximal chemical senses in a position of central influence for guiding and shaping human feeding and social interaction, two biological pillars that uphold survival of the individual and the species.

2 The Chemical Senses

2.1 Taste

Traditionally, we understand taste as a distinct oral sensory system or modality; it is well-known as one of the five senses. Taste, however, is inexorably linked to and integrated with olfaction and somesthesis (the skin senses) as we normally experience them from food in the mouth. This is both how the brain utilizes afferent taste signals and how we experience them in daily life. Hence, taste is one of several "proximal" chemosensory modalities that work in concert (see 2.4 The Proximal Chemical Senses). To separate taste from these other senses is to take it completely out of context. Whereas the traditional reductionist approach of isolating systems for study has been common among many laboratory scientists, this Element will explore these senses together because their comingling and merging is how we normally experience taste and the other upper airway senses, their perceptual constructs, and their associated behaviors.

These senses, while served by different nerves, are united as a functional group. For example, all taste stimuli also activate the somatosensory system, since the compounds must be carried on substrates or in solvents that are orally "felt." Furthermore, most sapid compounds have associated odors, presumably due to highly correlated volatile impurities and decomposition products. Where food is concerned, whenever taste is involved, smell and touch are also involved (as are vision and hearing to varying degrees). Further, the occasion of dining with another person (a topic examined later in this Element) may allow us to taste and smell the food, as well as smell the person with whom we dine, resulting in a complex integrated chemosensory "scene," which we chemically sample, analyze, and perceptually synthesize. Thus, when the term "taste" is used in this Element, it means taste as well as its epithelial sensory companions of touch and smell when pertinent, which is most of the time. Historically, taste, olfaction, and somesthesis were all conceived as being unified operationally as "the epithelial senses" of the upper airways and consequently were grouped together by Emil von Skramlik as "*der Niederen Sinnes*" (the lower [skin] senses)(Von Skramlik, 1926). These he contrasted with the distal "higher" senses of vision and hearing.

2.2 Olfaction

Olfaction is the sensation of airborne chemicals acting in the olfactory epithelium on olfactory receptors that lie high in the nasal cavity, almost between the eyes, and give rise to odor sensations. Typically, these compounds are small and volatile. There are, however, exceptions to this rule, such as when large nonvolatile molecules or particles are stirred-up with mechanical disturbance, such as by wind, or when they are given high energy, such as when cooking with oil. There are two air passageways that lead to the olfactory epithelium: one via the nostrils, called the orthonasal pathway; and one from inside the mouth and back up through the nasopharynx, called the retronasal pathway. Most food odors arising during eating and chewing are retronasal odors. Otherwise, almost all odors, including food odors, are orthonasal. Examples of olfactory qualities/ objects we experience include the odors of: wet dog fur, geranium flowers, cooked hotdogs, rotten eggs, babies' heads, motor oil, feces, and hundreds more. It is worth noting here that names for olfactory qualities are associated in many cultures (but not all) with object names, as in the preceding list, and are, therefore, less abstracted than qualities from other sensory modalities, such as red, sweet, or warm (Cain et al., 1998).

2.3 Chemical Somesthesis (Chemesthesis)

Chemical somesthesis or chemesthesis are the sensations of chemicals acting on the epidermis (skin) and epithelia (lining of the inside of the mouth, throat, nose, eyes, etc.) that give rise to myriad skin sensations, including warm, cool, hot, cold, tingle, tickle, itch, sting, burn, touch, light pressure, deep pressure, vibration, buzzing, and others. Chemicals have been identified that can elicit each of these sensations from skin and epithelia. Compounds that stimulate chemical somesthesis may be volatile and nonvolatile. Common food-based examples of chemesthetic compounds and their sensations are: the warmth and burn of capsaicin from chili peppers, the cool of menthol from mint, the irritation and sting of allyl isothiocyanate from horseradish, and the tingle and buzz of sanshool from Szechuan peppercorns. These compounds are thought to activate sensory neurons via action on ion channels in nerve endings within the skin and epithelia.

2.4 The Proximal Chemical Senses

All of our sensory systems can be divided into proximal and distal sensing groups. That is, whether they are activated when we are close to the stimulus source or whether they can be activated when we are far from the source, respectively. Taste and the skin senses are generally considered proximal sensory systems (for nonaquatic animals; Caprio et al., 1993), since contact or close proximity with the source of the stimuli is usually required to activate them. In contrast, olfaction, vision, and hearing can sense stimuli when the source is far away. Importantly, these three distal senses play a dual role and operate when a stimulus source is nearby as well. Thus, when food or people are near us, all of our senses can be activated at once. Olfaction has the further proximal sensory distinction of operating from within our mouths and bypass-ing our external nose via the retronasal air passage. This "retronasal" olfaction is a specialized proximal division of the olfactory sense that enables a different and more intimate perception of what has contacted the inside the mouth (Welge-Lussen et al., 2009). Thus, the sensory systems of the tongue with the oral and nasal cavities (the upper airways) integrate to create "flavor" as a proximal, polymodal, synthetic, and unified sensory experience, such as the flavor "gestalt" we experience when eating hot apple pie (Breslin, 2013; Breslin & Spector, 2008).

3 Perception

3.1 Taste

When we perceive a single taste (a qualia) such as the taste of a NaCl solution or a sucrose solution, the qualia may be subdivided into multiple perceptual attributes of: (1) quality (e.g., salty, sour, bitter, sweet, savory); (2) intensity (e.g., barely detectable, weak, moderate, strong); (3) location (e.g., taste on the tongue tip, back of tongue, soft palate, pharynx); (4) temporal (e.g., short-lived or enduring as an "aftertaste"); and (5) hedonic (e.g., pleasant or unpleasant). All of these five attributes are neurally encoded, so that when physiologists record from a taste-sensitive neuron (unit) either peripherally or centrally, it is unclear initially which attribute(s) are encoded within the signal or even of their sensory modality: taste, tactile, thermal, or some combination. Many taste responsive units are also tactile and thermal sensitive. Further, it may be impossible to understand taste to the exclusion of understanding touch, thermal, and even olfactory inputs, since they surely cooccur with every stimulation (Robinson, 1988). The fact that touch and thermal inputs are manipulated to be consistent across stimuli does not render them absent from what is encoded. There is a tendency among scientists to assume that a taste-sensitive unit carries information exclusively or predominantly about taste quality. But it is difficult to know the attribute(s) encoded within the signal simply from interpreting responses to a few stimuli.

Additionally, expectations of the perception will also guide interpretation of signals depending on whether we understand ourselves as tasting foods, medicines, or other people. Hence, it is inevitable that our responses to taste stimuli will only be normative and complete when we are fully aware of what we are tasting, so that expectations and interpretations may prime us for the stimulation (Kass et al., 2013; McGann, 2013). Understanding perception from the divisions of bottom up and top down do not quite make sense given that each controls the other from the outset, even before stimulation occurs in expectation of and according to our experience. Consider that top-down processing is clearly driven by previous experience. And while we might imagine that bottom-up processing is somehow purely the domain of receptor and afferent pathways, those too are modified as a result of their experience with stimuli and the constraints of the whole system. Bottom up and top down are oversimplifications of a vast array of reentrant neural subsystems. Those ideas represent a single time slice in an ongoing network of constant change. As such, these levels of analysis are illusory. Inevitably, the results of any animal or network-based experiment will incorporate some knowledge of what was – rather than merely what is – the state of the organism. It might be meaningful to describe a single experience as "mostly top down" or "mostly bottom up," but that experience has now changed the system leaving it newly modified for the stimuli that will follow.

3.2 Quality

Since Aristotle and even earlier, taste has been divided into major qualities (McBurney & Gent, 1979). These are most famously sour, salty, sweet, and bitter. Although early understandings of taste included astringent and pungent as taste qualities, these were later excluded as they could be elicited from nongustatory epithelia. Astringency can be classified as a somatosensation, related to oral qualities of mouth feel (e.g., lubricity, rheology, and tribology)

(Breslin et al., 1993; Green, 1993). But because these sensations can also be elicited from taste epithelia and, in particular, gain special access to neurons within the epithelium via taste pores, the roles of tactile, astringent, lubricating, fatty, and pungent sensations on taste may perhaps merge these modalities perceptually to some degree (see 3.4 Die Niederen Sinnes). A quality of taste, such as sweetness, is ultimately a perception that must be consciously and widely recognized as a distinct qualitative experience. For example, "metallic taste" (the experience of licking metallic zinc, copper, and some other metals) has been debated as to whether it is a unique taste, a somatosensation, or a combination of the two, but presently it is not clear to what sensory modality it belongs – that the sensation is experienced, however, is not in question (Lawless et al., 2004).

The main four taste qualities might not be the only taste qualities we can perceive. In fact, there might be a great many more. We tend to focus on these four because they are very common sensations we can clearly experience in isolation: the taste of acidic fruit juices, the taste of salt, the taste of honey, and the taste of medicines. Also, we tend to focus on the four main taste qualities because they can stimulate high maximum intensities; that is, we can experience all of them as strongly intense. Curiously, maximum perceived intensities differ from stimulus to stimulus and from quality to quality, so their robustness and salience differs. For example, of all of the high potency noncaloric sweeteners used to make diet sodas, none can reach a maximum sweetness intensity as high as that of the sugars sucrose or fructose. There are also taste qualities that have lower maximum intensities than sour, salty, sweet, and bitter; they are, therefore, less salient and garner less attention. Taste qualities that have lower maximum intensities include savory or umami (the taste of glutamate mixed with IMP or GMP), maltooligosaccharide taste (the taste of starch decomposition products or small glucose polymers), and nonsalty/nonbitter cation tastes (a subquality of calcium and potassium salts) (Chen et al., 2009; Lapis et al., 2017; Tordoff, 2001). There may even be tastes that have an intensity so low that we are not fully aware they have a unique quality, such as the taste of fatty acids from triglycerides and the taste of water. The latter two might be detectable and able to influence our perceived hedonics and preference for substances sampled without eliciting a unique conscious quality.

All of these taste sensations can be mapped into a theoretical taste space that is all inclusive of our perceptual experiences. Within this space will reside regions we may label with particular qualities, but this space will most certainly have more than four regions. It may have dozens of regions, some of which elicit taste sensations that have no quality. This is because some tastes may only influence our physiology or our affective processing and liking, yet they reside within this space. Taste space may also bleed into, intersect with, or be bent and warped by tactile and thermal spaces. Hence, we may need a partial return to Aristotle's claim that astringency and pungency are tastes. There will also be stimuli that occupy several regions of the taste space at once because they elicit multiple qualities. There are infamous examples of multiquality stimuli, such as the "sweeteners" saccharin and acesulfame, which elicit both sweetness and bitterness. But the most diverse multiquality stimuli are salts, such as NH_4Cl, which can elicit three or four different qualities of taste at once (Murphy, Cardello, & Brand, 1981).

All taste stimulations by nutrients or toxins likely have physiological and metabolic consequences. The three caloric macronutrients (carbohydrates/ sugars, fats/fatty acids, proteins/amino acids) likely generate taste-triggered metabolic signals that prepare the body to process the incoming calories and also to drive liking and ingestion. All three generate taste signals, and for carbohydrates, there is evidence of metabolic priming (Mandel & Breslin, 2012). For the bitter-tasting toxins, especially when strongly bitter, there are physiological consequences that limit intake and absorption and can also induce feelings of nausea (Peyrot des Gachons et al., 2011). For sour stimuli, our inherent attraction and repulsion is determined by concentration (we tend to prefer lower concentrations [except for children, who can enjoy very high concentrations]) and contextual food cues such as presence in fruit (sweet paired) or fermented foods (savory paired). The physiological consequences of sour taste, however, are unknown at this time. For stimuli such as maltooli- gosaccharides, fatty acids, nonsodium cations, and water, there are metabolic consequences that arise even in the absence of clear and specific taste qualities. For example, maltooligosaccharides elicit an early insulin response from oral stimulation (Mandel & Breslin, 2012), even though their malty taste is weak at best (Breslin, Beauchamp, & Pugh, 1996; Lapis et al., 2017).

3.3 Hedonics and Preferences

Taste sensations elicit innate reactions of like and dislike depending on whether they signal nutrients or toxins, respectively. Hence, we are born liking and wanting to ingest sweet-tasting substances and disliking and wanting to reject bitter-tasting substances. We hypothesize that these taste-triggered facial reflexes are the foundation of human emotions via the facial efference theory of emotion (See 6 Emotions).

Our enjoyment, liking, and preferences for foods are also subject to social context and experiences. Foremost, the post–ingestive consequences of ingesting foods with caloric benefit or toxic effects strongly influence whether we will come to seek out these foods in the future via conditioned taste preference (Sclafani & Nissenbaum, 1988) or avoid them via conditioned taste aversion (Garcia, Hankins, & Rusiniak, 1976; Garcia et al., 1985), respectively. This plasticity in hedonics or liking allows humans to perceive certain chemosensory attributes, such as flavor, as unchanging, yet whether we seek these flavors or avoid them depends on their associations (Birch et al., 1990; Scalera, 2002).

Social context also plays a major role in our relation to food ingestion and liking. Rodents learn about safe flavors to eat from the mixture of flavor and hydrogen sulfide on the breath of other "demonstrator" animals (Galef & Kennett, 1987; Galef & Whiskin, 1997). We too learn from the habits and conversations of others about what is both safe to eat and good to eat. For example, we may learn to like foods of a culture different from our own that at first seemed unpleasant. Here, the practice of so many others and observation of their eating habits may help to teach us that the food is safe, nutritious, even delicious. This may also occur at a smaller scale from the feedback of others around a table either positive or negative regarding a particular food or dish. The flavor that we perceive is the combination of all oral stimulus sensations and retronasal inputs, as well as visual and auditory inputs. These may all be combined to yield our overall perception of the food's flavor. The multimodal sensory integration that generates flavor may be the most complicated sensory integration of which humans are capable, but whether we enjoy these flavors is largely based on our history with them.

Expectations influence the flavor we perceive as well. We come to expect a flavor based on verbal information. That is, labeling, marketing, and conversations inform us of what we are about to receive. This cues a mental flavor engram against which oral samples are compared. If the flavor memory or engram is not a close match to what we perceive, then we may perceive it as both "wrong" and unpalatable. As a *gedanken* exercise, imagine being offered a home-prepared tomato juice that was actually a pulpy orange juice that was dyed red. The mismatch from what was expected and what was perceived might be shocking and cause the opinion that the tomato juice was terrible, even though it may be perfectly pleasant tasting orange juice. Color may also lead to the perception of flavors that are not chemically present due to expectations. Thus, a sweet-and-sour-tasting, citrus-smelling beverage is ambiguously citrus fruit flavored, but may be perceived as lime flavored if green or grapefruit flavored if pink (Stillman, 1993).

3.4 Die Niederen Sinnes

Emil von Skramlik referred to the epithelial receptor systems as *die niederen Sinnes* or "the lower senses" (Von Skramlik, 1926). These he collectively believed were part of one overarching system of receptors embedded within an epithelial sheet that functioned together. Thus, chemicals, material substances (foods and beverages), temperatures, breaths, and so on all impact the epithelia at once and are processed collectively by the epithelial sheet and the brain. The tactile receptors, the thermal-sensing free nerve endings, the chemosensors, the nociceptors, as well as the taste and the olfactory receptors are all embedded within a continuous epithelial sheet, albeit not all in the same location. He envisioned that they operate as a sort of epithelial ecosystem, each perhaps occupying a different niche functionally but all working together as part of an integrated whole. There is also an epithelial cartographic component in that we tend to be able to identify the location of most epithelial stimulations. This conceptualization of the epithelium as an überorgan makes sense as this is how the physical world impacts us and it also happens to be how integrative areas of our brains, such as the insular cortices, process inputs from our upper airways. Hence, von Skramlik's conceptualization supports our use of taste perception as part of the proximal chemical senses in toto.

3.5 Perceiving Food and People: Scene Analysis

Unlike the role of conditioned taste preferences and conditioned taste aversions in which our attitude and affective processing for a food is altered by association, we may also come to have altered stimulus perception through learning and experience. The ability to "see" or perceive what we previously could not is a form of perceptual learning. The stimulus is not changing nor is its impact on our receptors. Rather, perceptual learning is a guided use of attention to features and attributes that permits us to focus on them. We do not perceive what we do not attend to, a phenomenon known as "inattentive blindness" (Lorig, 2012; Zucco, Priftis, & Stevenson, 2015). Experience and training usually serve to make us "experts" at perceiving, whether it is to see densities in mammograms or detect subtle off-notes in wines. As is typical of perceptual learning, once we learn the skill of guiding our attention to perceive features, it is difficult to stop attending to these features. Thus, once we learn that there is the necessary hint of cat urine odor in a fresh orchard peach, we will always know when it is there; just as once we learn to see and appreciate the subtle undertones of pinks, blues, greens and yellows in various shades of "the color white," we will see these hues in the whites around us in wall colors, clouds, book pages, papers, lights, and so forth.

As we gradually become familiar with the flavors and aromas of favorite foods and dishes as well as the fragrance and body odor of friends and acquaintances, we come to build our flavor and aroma engrams, which helps us know when foods are ready, ripe, and prepared correctly. This also provides a great advantage in recognizing when something has gone wrong, such as when food may be spoiled or when a friend may be sick. The perceptual learning about the proximal chemosensory signals of foods and friends and the building of their engrams enables us to identify situations that may be safe or harmful, and to be prepared for either outcome.

It is well recognized that humans have an extraordinary expertise for human faces and for facial recognition (Haxby, Hoffman, & Gobbini, 2000). We are quite simply experts at this – all of us. Although there may be an inborn preparedness to have this expertise, I believe this is another example of perceptual learning in which we stare into people's faces every day of our lives, and from this learning comes expertise. I believe humans have a similar expertise for food flavors. We eat food several times a day almost every day of our lives. Food flavors can be extremely complicated both chemically and perceptually. Yet we have mastery of the food flavors we experience with regularity. I believe our expertise for food flavors may even rival that of dogs' abilities to smell body odors of other dogs and animals.

Science has a strong tendency to isolate and identify. This has also been a standard part of perceptual science. Fortunately, more recent trends in perceptional research, and vision research in particular, have recognized that isolation is not the way in which our senses work. This Element makes a point of linking taste (per se), smell, and somatosensory stimulation to understand our perception of flavor and foods because these systems are not isolated. But, perhaps surprisingly, our discussion here has also been somewhat limited in showing the context of flavor stimulation. In the last decade, visual science has recognized the importance of scene analysis (Enns & Rensink, 1990; Wolfe et al., 2011). The scene analysis approach to chemosensory perception needs to be applied to flavor and all of chemosensory research as well. For instance, our familiarity and expertise with food flavors and also with human odors is useful in social situations in which we are around multiple dishes and multiple people. There exists in these situations a chemosensory scene that must be analyzed to enable us to determine the source and identity of chemicals. The task is made easier by the fact that not all objects are equiintense or equidistant from us. In addition, we are not static relative to the objects. Thus, we talk with one person and then another, or we may bring a food closer to us and into our mouths one at a time. Once a food or beverage is in our mouths, they can stimulate retronasal olfaction as well as taste and chemesthetic stimulation, which makes identification and recognition much easier. Our sensory systems and our brain may also be organized to process edible signals and social signals separately (Bender et al., 2009; Small et al., 2005; Welge-Lussen et al., 2009). There are many chemical cues, however, that are common to both foods and humans, and how we parse them perceptually will be based upon our expectations of what we are experiencing, such as cheese versus human feet. Note again that olfactory quality is intimately linked to source object, at least in Western culture, resulting in odd ambiguities of either smelling like stinky feet or good cheese.

3.6 Art and Gastronomy

Art is the skillfully executed, emotionally evocative, perceptual abstraction of the familiar and unfamiliar. Art is ancient; earliest observations of cave art appeared over 40,000 years ago. Art is ubiquitous and highly valued; every culture has some form of art and in all modern developed societies there are public art museums, theaters, and concert halls. People and civilizations invest in art as much as they do in gold and other precious metals. Art is a reflective and refined abstraction of our lives, a way to see ourselves in a new light, with a new perspective. It is a lens through which we can look into a mirror, or perhaps a mirror shard, and try to understand ourselves better. Art involves all of the senses and can take virtually any form; it can be flat, three dimensional, temporary, semipermanent, static or kinetic, paintings or movies, it can be inanimate or live, it can be music, dance, or literature, and can take place or be positioned anywhere. Art can be presented in any medium, and for the proximal chemical senses, it is most commonly presented in the medium of food . . . food and flavor as art.

Since gastronomy is the art of cooking, excellent gastronomy is not just food that tastes delicious, but food that invites you to appreciate that it is unusual, better, skillful, and draws in the consumer to wonder how is it different from the everyday and what makes it so unusual. Gastronomy can be interesting, unfamiliar, surprising, even shocking. But as is true of most art, gastronomy should cause the perceiver (or consumer) to be reflective: of the food, the flavors, the sources of foods and flavors, the scene, the culture, and the idea of how we relate to the world around us. And while gastronomy can challenge our perceptions and ideas of flavor and familiarity, comfortable flavors of "home cooking" sustain us just as the folk art on the refrigerator does.

Summary: Our perceptions of tastes and the chemical stimuli of the upper airways are highly integrated multimodal signals. So much so that it may be difficult to separate modalities from one another. How we come to perceive flavors and tastes, foods and friends, is highly malleable and will be based upon our familiarity, consequence learning, contextual learning, and perceptual learning and experience. The more familiar we are, the greater our expertise. When it comes to food flavors, all humans are extreme experts. This is useful for chemosensory scene analysis when we are surrounded by foods and people and their signals are blended and mixed into a great mélange. The patchiness of signals and our ability to move through this dynamically, as well as to put objects into our mouths, enables us to make perceptual "sense" of the scene.

4 Nutrition

Taste plays a fundamental role for nutritional health (energy, water, and nutrient balance) by guiding food and water ingestion and priming the body for the metabolism of what is ingested (Breslin, 2013). We can taste the building blocks of all three macronutrients, carbohydrates, proteins, and fats (sugars, amino acids, fatty acids), as well as water, minerals (Na, Cl, K, Ca, Mg, Zn, Fe) and some essential vitamins (ascorbic acid [vitamin C]) (Breslin & Spector, 2008; Schiffman & Dackis, 1975). Since water, energy balance, and proper nutrition are required for life, the sensory guides to these nutrients, taste and the proximal chemical senses, are consequently critical for life. This is especially true for foraging omnivores and other species that must identify and select their foods. In contrast, the more rarified and predetermined the diet, such as in obligate carnivores or the more extreme monovores (e.g., pandas) (Zhao et al., 2010), the less the chemical senses are required (Li et al., 2005). Thus, the chemical senses are needed by humans to guide dietary selection and intake, as well as to guide nutrient processing and metabolism in a world where food options are multitudinous and globally varied.

4.1 Taste Is Useful for Food Recognition

The taste system, together with olfaction, serves to conduct a chemical analysis of food (sensory chromatography) to detect and semiquantitatively represent the levels of a variety of nutrients and toxins (Breslin, 2013). Chewing both softens and reduces the size of foods that will be swallowed in the form of a minced, moistened food bolus and also releases compounds and nutrients from within the food into saliva so we can taste and smell them (Taylor, 1996). Most everything we taste is water soluble to some degree and needs to be solubilized to be tasted. Either the food's natural juices or our saliva supplies this solvent. Whereas most readers will be familiar with four or five "basic" tastes, it is more instructive to consider them from the context of the information they provide about nutrients (Breslin, 2013). Sweet taste allows us to detect the presence of common sugars in fruits and other foods. Salty taste allows us to detect certain minerals, especially sodium salts, in foods and from salt deposits. Savory taste (also known as umami taste) allows us to detect amino acids, especially glutamate and aspartate, from fermented, cooked, and dried foods in which the proteins are broken down. Sour taste allows us to detect acids, which are not necessary nutrients, except for ascorbic acid (Vitamin C) and certain essential fatty acids (all long chain fatty acids that have very low water solubility). Sour taste could also be used as a marker of both fermentation and fruit ripeness, especially when there is balance between sweetness and sourness. Sour taste may also be a warning against overly acidic foods that could cause tissue damage. The taste of maltooligosaccharides (MOS) (small polymers of glucose), water taste, mineral taste, and fat taste are examples of other qualities of taste that have been suggested as nutrient indicators and for which there is either some physiological or perceptual evidence (Besnard, Passilly-Degrace, & Khan, 2016; Lapis et al., 2017; Running, Craig, & Mattes, 2015; Tordoff, 2001). Bitter taste is discussed in the following paragraphs as a marker of toxins (see 4.4 Taste Allows Us to Avoid Poisons) (Peyrot des Gachons et al., 2011).

4.2 The Organ of Taste

Within the oral cavity, taste arises from several sensory epithelial fields comprised of the edges and dorsal surface of the tongue (what people can see when you stick out your tongue), the posterior surface of the tongue that bends down the throat (the genoux of the tongue), the soft palate (the roof of the mouth directly above the genoux of the tongue and behind the hard bony palate behind the incisors), and the pharynx (the back of the throat, typically what hurts during a sore throat) (Breslin & Huang, 2006). Embedded within these epithelial sensory fields are the microorgans of taste, the taste buds. A taste bud is a microscopic, multicellular, rosebud-shaped organ comprised of approximately 80 to 100 cells that is open and exposed to the oral cavity and foods via a hole in the epithelium called a "taste pore." The tongue and mouth are covered with thousands of these rosebud-shaped microorgans. The heterogeneous cells of the taste bud are made up of several different types differing in function and morphology (shape) and each typically expressing one class of receptor (e.g., toxin or carbohydrate receptors) (Chaudhari & Roper, 2010). The various electrically active receptor cells express different receptor types, including members of the ion channel class (ionotropic) and the GTP-Binding-Protein Coupled Receptor (GPCR) class (metabotropic). It is believed that each taste bud can respond to stimuli that we perceive as sweet, savory, bitter, salty, and sour, and thus contains the cells types and their corresponding receptors to enable this perception. These receptors are presently divided into two subclasses of metabotropic receptors (T1Rs for sweet and savory tastes and T2Rs for all bitter taste) and two subclasses of ionotropic receptors (sensitive to metal ions for salty and to protons [acids] for sour) (Kinnamon, 1988). The cells within a taste bud are also thought to communicate among themselves and engage in first stage electrocellular coding of stimuli that is passed along to the nervous system, predominantly via ATP signaling (Herness et al., 2005). Within the epithelia of the tongue, taste buds reside within specialized bumps called papillae that serve a variety of functions including creating microenvironments and allowing oral glandular secretions to mix with stimuli (Gurkan & Bradley, 1987). Within the soft palate and pharynx there are no papillae; here, taste buds reside within "smooth" epithelia. Although taste receptor fields of the oral cavity are slightly specialized for select stimuli, each quality of taste can be elicited from every epithelial receptor field (Sato, Endo, & Tomita, 2002). For example, sweet, sour, salty, bitter, and savory tastes can easily be demonstrated to oneself as arising from the tip of the tongue. This last statement comes with the caveat that genetic-based individual differences are the rule rather than the exception, and some people will not be able to experience certain bitter or savory taste stimuli.

Beyond the mouth, taste receptor cells appear in a variety of locations throughout the gastrointestinal (GI) tract and upper (nasal and sinus) and lower (lungs) airways (Behrens & Meyerhof, 2010). Here, however, they are distinguished by several features: first, they do not give rise to conscious taste sensations; second, they do not appear within buds but rather appear as solitary cells labeled solitary chemosensory cells (SCCs); and third, they serve to aid in processing, removing, neutralizing, or digesting the activating stimuli (Finger et al., 2003). Thus, SCCs regulate metabolism, endocrine function, secretions, transport, elimination, and immune reactions to stimuli and to the stimulus-generating entities, be they foods, organic particles, or microbes (Depoortere, 2014; Howitt et al., 2016; Lee, Depoortere, & Hatt, 2018; Sternini, Anselmi, & Rozengurt, 2008).

4.3 Taste Helps Regulate Metabolism

The stimulation of oral taste receptors causes neural and humoral signals to be directed to the metabolic organs, such as the pancreas and liver, which prepares them for incoming nutrients (Powley & Berthoud, 1985; Teff, Devine, & Engelman, 1995; Teff, Mattes, & Engelman, 1991). For example, insulin-dependent carbohydrates like starches and table sugar (sucrose) cause a small release of insulin prior to the absorption of the sugar into the blood (Mandel & Breslin, 2012). The orally triggered preabsorptive insulin is critical in keeping blood sugar low following a meal and accomplishes this with relatively less insulin – this is the regulatory metabolic ideal. The logic underlying this event is that by releasing small amounts of insulin preabsorptively, blood glucose begins to be taken up from the blood by tissues at the same time that glucose is beginning to rise in the blood from absorbed food. This lowers the peak blood glucose level achieved after the meal and less insulin is released overall. This is highly beneficial, as excess blood sugar and excess insulin in the blood cause eventual vascular disease and shortened life span (Maddigan, Feeny, & Johnson, 2005). Beyond carbohydrates, all macronutrients and minerals that we taste may induce similar anticipatory physiological signals. Thus, taste appears to be critical for anticipating the nutrients that are going to be absorbed (Breslin, 2018). Note that this is important for species, such as humans, in which the diet is highly varied. In animals for which the diet is nutritionally constant, such as carnivores that swallow their prey whole (e.g., sea lions), there is no need to evaluate and anticipate absorbed nutrients orally under the presumption that lack of dietary variety allows the body to know what is swallowed (Jiang et al., 2012).

4.4 Taste Allows Us to Avoid Poisons

Just as important as identifying, ingesting, and anticipating nutrients in the diet for survival is the identification and avoidance of toxins. Many bitter-tasting compounds are poisonous at high doses. The bitterness inherent in foods is not poisonous at the levels we ingest them, but would be at higher, more bitter-tasting levels. It is not a perfect system, as many poisons are not bitter tasting and several bitter-tasting compounds are not poisonous (Nissim, Dagan-Wiener, & Niv, 2017). But the majority of plant-, animal-, and fungal-based toxins taste bitter. There are approximately twenty-five bitter taste receptor genes in each person's genome, for which we are typically heterozygous – carrying two alleles for most of them that may differ in their responsiveness to bitter taste ligands (Kim et al., 2005; Kim et al., 2004). Thus, each of us may be capable of producing at least fifty bitter taste receptors. There are several alleles of each bitter taste gene; so, within a small population there may be hundreds of different bitter taste receptors making the poisoning of a community all the more difficult (especially a community that eats together, i.e., "communally"; see 5 Social Interactions). It is of the highest biological importance not to be poisoned, as a single exposure to a potent toxin can result in death. Therefore, evolution has assured that it is very difficult for people to ingest foods that are very strongly bitter tasting (Glendinning, Tarre, & Asaoka, 1999; Mattes, 1997; Sandell & Breslin, 2006). Moreover, we have physiological anticipatory responses to strong bitter tastes, opposite of our physiological responses to macronutrients. First, strong bitter tastes trigger feelings of nausea, which are as punishing as pain sensations (Peyrot des Gachons et al., 2011). This causes us to stop eating whatever is strongly bitter tasting. Second, strong bitter tastes cause our stomach muscles to stop contracting rhythmically and to twitch chaotically, effectively trapping the food in our stomach and preparing for regurgitation if necessary (Peyrot des Gachons et al., 2011).

4.5 Taste Is for Microbial Identification, the Formation of the Gut Microbiome, and Defense against Food Pathogens (Fermentation and Spoiling)

Taste has the unusual property of detecting the destruction of macronutrients and ribonucleic acids (RNAs) into components. For example, when food is either slow cooked or fermented, the proteins in cells will break down into its amino acids, of which glutamate is the most common nonessential amino acid (Giacometti, 1979), and the RNAs in cells will break down into component ribonucleotides and ribonucleosides (Yamaguchi & Ninomiya, 2000). We have a taste receptor (T1R1/T1R3) that responds particularly well to the concurrent presence of both glutamate and certain ribonucleosides, such as inosine or guanosine, common in cellular transfer RNAs and ribosomal RNAs (Li, 2009; Li et al., 2002). Although there are foods that are naturally high in glutamate and the ribonucleosides inosine and guanosine, such as mushrooms, these components will typically only be high in foods that have either been slow cooked for long periods or fermented. Since fermentation long predates the use of cooking (Dudley, 2014), we can presume this taste, which we call savory or umami, was initially related to fermentation. In fact, our love of fermentation may have predisposed us to like and to create these tastes from cooking (c.f. Wrangham, 2009).

For every type of food that humans eat, there is a version that we eat in fermented form, and there is no human culture that does not eat fermented foods, making fermented foods ubiquitous (Katz, 2012). There are three very important reasons to eat fermented foods. First, the foods are essentially pre-digested and, therefore, are easier to eat and are more nutritious (Wrangham, 2009). Second, we cannot survive in the world without a healthy gut microbiome and fermented foods contain friendly, probiotic, gut-colonizing bacteria (Katz, 2012). Early life exposure to them can make children healthier (Lenfestey & Neu, 2017). These bacteria provide us with nutritionally important short-chain fatty acids, they digest foods for us that we have difficulty digesting (resistant starches), they synthesize essential vitamins (thiamine, biotin, riboflavin, folate, pantothenic acid, vitamin B12), and they outcompete and prevent infections from invading microbes (Sun & Chang, 2014). Third, food can spoil and create opportunities for microbial pathogens. Many of these microbial pathogens cannot be detected by taste or smell and can be lethal, including clostridium botulinum, salmonella, staphylococcus, listeria, campylobacter, and common causes of dysentery – such as shigella. But in a controlled fermentation, the good microbes are so successful and abundant that pathogenic microbes cannot thrive, assuring the food is safe to eat (Katz, 2012). Hence, there are some ancient and strong evolutionary forces to love fermented foods, which humans most certainly do.

The chemical senses detect stimuli outside the body with exteroceptors as well as inside the body with enteroceptors. In addition to taste receptor expression in the oral cavity, which gives rise to conscious taste perception, there is expression of taste receptors (and other chemosensory receptors) throughout the body. Taste receptors are expressed throughout the GI tract from the mouth to the pharynx, to the stomach and small and large intestines. They are also expressed within all major metabolic tissues, including the liver, pancreas, thyroid, brain, adipocytes, and lungs. Taste receptors that detect stimuli and nutrients in the mouth and GI tract prior to being absorbed into the body are referred to as exteroceptors; their function is to detect what compounds are about to enter the body. Taste receptors that detect stimuli and nutrients inside the body are referred to as enteroceptors; their function is to let tissues know what nutrients and other compounds are coursing through our blood and may need to be metabolically utilized or stored (Berthoud, 2002).

Summary: Taste and the proximal chemosensory systems are fundamental to identifying nutrients and toxins in foods, motivating us to eat or reject them, respectively, establishing a healthy gut microbiome by driving us to eat fermented foods, and preparing our metabolic tissues for what is about to enter the body so that what enters will be processed quickly and efficiently.

5 Social Interactions

5.1 Chemical Communication

While not typically considered when addressing the sense of taste, a growing literature shows the proximal chemical senses are very important to human social interactions. When we engage others socially, we are close to them. So close that we smell them. Thus, humans in many cultures strive to smell pleasant and inoffensive. They wash before gathering, use perfumed deodorants and shampoos, brush their teeth, use mouthwash, and wear fragrances and colognes. The goal is not necessarily to hide one's own odor, although this has been proposed as a reason for perfume use (Stoddart, 1990), but rather to be chemically pleasing.

There is a common belief that too much of one's own odor or unwashed body odor, hair/scalp odor, and oral odor would be off-putting to others.

It is also the case that when humans gather socially either in groups or in pairs, they frequently eat and drink together. In an anthropological and evolutionary sense, this might seem strange. Food was often scarce for our ancestors, and keeping food and food sources to oneself would have had some obvious survival value. On the other hand, sharing food would be (and is) a key means of cementing the social relationships necessary for survival and reproduction (Jaeggi & Gurven, 2013). It is quite possible that as our ancestors killed large prey animals and cooked them, the hunting party, their families, and perhaps others took part in the bounty – especially since there would have been few means of storing excess food, although what was stored would probably ferment (Katz, 2012). It is likely that we have held on to some of the social sides of this behavior. In modern times we may engage with others for a formal meal or lighter fare, such as snacks, hors d'oeuvres, and drinks. No matter the type of food interaction, we are close to each other when we eat; close enough to smell each other's food. Inevitably, the smell and taste of the foods intermingle with the smell of other people into a larger proximal chemical and chemosensory mélange. This complex and dynamic chemical cloud is sampled and analyzed by our upper airway sensory modalities and the afferent signals are sent to the brain to make sense of the scene by creating chemosensory objects: foods, dishes, drinks, wine, coffee, yourself, others, the room or space, etc. Furthermore, this scene is not static but changes over time, and the objects within the scene are relational: I am dining with you, your dish, my dish, nearby diners and their dishes. It is the relational nature of the chemosensory scene that both guides and strengthens human social interactions.

5.2 Food and Sex

Taste and the proximal chemical senses play an essential role in both survival of the individual as well as survival of the species via their impact on food selection, nutrition, mate selection, and sex. There are many nonhuman species that smell and taste each other, including mammals. For those of us familiar with domestic dogs and cats, think of the frequency with which they lick us. It is easier for us to understand animals sniffing each other than licking because humans tend not to lick others as much. Dogs, on the other hand, lick other dogs' faces and mouths as well as their genitalia. Whereas the tactile and grooming components of dogs licking faces has been commented on (Siniscalchi et al., 2018), it is also clear that if there is licking, there is tasting. Yet, we are not sure to what degree actual tasting guides or motivates mammalian social licking, except in cases where licks contact pheromones and obvious responses ensue, such as the Flehmen response (Allen, Yovovich, & Wilmers, 2016). For invertebrates and for most aquatic animals, however, tasting is critical to social recognition of gender, mating status, and possibly species recognition. In fish, the bile salts released into the water provide abundant information about conspecifics as well as about other species in the area via olfaction and gustation (Buchinger, Li, & Johnson, 2014).

Among flies, most studied are the Drosophilids, they clearly taste each other's bodies, legs, and genitals with their proboscis, which is a retractable drinking tube terminating in lips covered with taste receptors – an analog to a tongue (Quinn & Greenspan, 1984). The information gained when flies "lick" each other is thought to include the lickee's genus and species, their gender, their prior history with the licker, and whether they have recently copulated (Billeter et al., 2009; Fan et al., 2013). All of this is important gustatory information related to their compatibility, ability to mate, and likelihood to increase one's own fitness when mating. Flies also eat socially; when food is discovered by one, a chemical signal is generated called an "aggregation pheromone" that attracts others to the food where they will communally feed, meet, possibly fight, and likely mate (Bartelt, Schaner, & Jackson, 1985; Chen et al., 2002; Greenspan & Ferveur, 2000). There is even an influence of sexual behavior on appetites and nutrition. For example, when flies (Drosophila) mate, there is chemical communication transmitted via peptides in semen (e.g., sex peptide) detected by receptors within female genitals that profoundly alters the females' nutritional preferences, especially for dietary protein (taken as yeast) in order to produce offspring (Bowman & Tatar, 2016; Tsuda & Aigaki, 2016).

5.2.1 Human Compatibility: Mate Selection and Bond Maintenance

Proximal chemosensory cues are also crucial for human social relationships. The idea that people can be socially compatible is generally regarded as the *sine qua non* for developing friendships, bonding, mating, and reproducing. Although we may place social status, income, religion, political affiliation, physical constitution, visual appearance, intelligence, personality, or sense of humor as high on our compatibility list of traits, chemosensory compatibility appears to be at its root. People tend to bond with individuals whose odor and possibly also taste they enjoy (when applicable: see 5.2.3 Why Do Humans Kiss?). The human leukocyte antigen (HLA) status ties immune function to individual body odor "fingerprint," as one's HLA status genetically imparts both individual immunity and body odor (Beauchamp & Yamazaki, 1997; 2002; Wedekind et al., 1995). We tend to like, be attracted to, be satisfied by, and bond with those who are dissimilar to us in HLA status – connoting both a difference in immunogenetics and a difference in body odor type (Beauchamp & Yamazaki, 1997; Jacob et al., 2002; Wedekind et al., 1995). This preference is bounded, however, so that we are neither attracted to immediate family members nor to those who are extremely different from ourselves (Havlicek & Roberts, 2009; Jacob et al., 2002). It is unclear at this time whether HLA generates stimuli (thought to be peptide fragments) that present in the oral cavity and can be tasted by others.

Given that it is the females rather than the males who choose mates in heterosexual couples (Cox & Le Boeuf, 1977; Jacob et al., 2002; Janetos, 1980), it is important to note that women report a partner's odor as their most important sensory attribute, even more so than their appearance or "looks" (Herz, 2008). Women who partner with men who are different in HLA status report greater satisfaction with the relationship and greater sexual satisfaction, and are less likely to pursue additional partner sexual relationships compared with women who partner with men of more similar HLA type (Kromer et al., 2016). Thus, the odor of the partner is not only important for selection but also in bond maintenance and the relationship.

Somewhat related to social odor, there is a chemosensory organ in the nose of many mammals that appears specialized for chemical social communication and is found in the anterior nasal septum. This vomeronasal organ (VNO) is specialized for detecting semiochemicals (conspecific social signals) that can be volatile as well as nonvolatile (Keverne, 1999). The nonvolatile compounds are delivered to the nasal septum by pressing the nose into the source, such as into body regions, into urine, or both during nasal–genital contact (Wysocki et al., 1985; Wysocki, Wellington, & Beauchamp, 1980). The chemical signals received by the VNO are neurally transmitted to the brain and are important for mating but may also be involved with detecting predator urine and with conspecific aggression (Keverne, 1999; Papes, Logan, & Stowers, 2010). The VNO is not considered a distal sense organ but rather functions as a more intimate proximal chemosensory system. It should be noted that adult humans do not appear to have a functional VNO, although humans do possess a vestigial VNO pit (the cul-de-sac that forms the entryway to the sensory epithelium of the organ) in our nasal septum at the location where other species possess them (Meredith, 2001). But this does not mean that humans are without pheromones, as they may act via the primary olfactory epithelium (Grammer, Fink, & Neave, 2005; Stern & McClintock, 1998). The clearest examples of human pheromones are the axial (underarm) cues that women use to induce menstrual synchrony with other cycling women (Stern & McClintock, 1998). Furthermore, despite not having a functioning VNO, humans regularly engage in VNO-associated social behaviors, such as pressing our mouths and noses into others' bodies, see section 5.2.3 Why Do Humans Kiss?

5.2.2 Social Eating and Food Sharing

Taste clearly contributes to the compatibility and bonding between people when they are eating socially. Sharing food necessitates a form of intimacy because we are feeding the other and sharing tastes and flavors. This is the basis of the religious practice of sharing bread and wine in Christian Communion (Eucharist), a practice of intimate food sharing that is designed to build community both physically and spiritually. A great percentage of human socializing occurs over food, whether with community, family, friends, or mates. So much so that those who experience chemosensory loss and consequently lose interest in food, tend not to eat meals socially at restaurants as frequently, which results in a major decrement in their quality of social life and can result in depression (Toller, 1999). Clearly, taste and smell are necessary guides to food preferences (Mattes, 1994; Schiffman & Dackis, 1975) and, therefore, to compatibility during social eating. Some readers may have experience eating with others whose food preferences are markedly different from their own. It would be awkward to have a close or intimate relationship with someone who never wants to eat the same foods as you; how would you cook or choose a restaurant? And, though it would be convenient, it would also be strange to eat with someone who only ever wanted to eat exactly what we eat. As with body odor, we prefer those who are similar to us but not identical in their taste preferences. Perhaps food preferences serve as a proxy for genetic status via the heterogeneity of taste and odor receptors and their influence on our food preferences.

Eating with another person provides opportunities for sharing and bonding over food that are dependent on our proximal chemical senses. For example, we can evaluate and discuss the sensory properties of each other's foods providing comparisons of similarity of likes and dislikes. Hence meal comments might include, "I can't believe you are going to eat that!" expressing extreme dissimilarity and potential revulsion of the other's choices. In contrast, if food is left on another's plate and we desire it, we might ask, **"Are you going to eat that?"** connoting approval of the food choices and exploring their desire to share food and their social boundaries, as well as reinforcing preexisting bonds and familiarity. The social eating scenario is an ideal situation for evaluating one another for sensory, genetic, emotional, and social compatibility. Although the evaluations of each other in this situation are highly multifactorial, the proximal chemical senses play a pivotal role in determining how we relate to the other person and their food choices. In fact, conversations about food (what to eat, when to eat, where to eat, what groceries to shop for, how to cook, who will cook, etc.) seem to comprise a disproportionate percentage of our conversations due to the intrinsically social aspect of eating for them.

5.2.3 Why Do Humans Kiss?

Kissing is almost ubiquitous for humans, but there is relatively little evidence suggesting the origin for this behavior. Kissing can be a sign of friendship, love, and greeting. In a great many cultures, we kiss hands, cheeks, lips, foreheads, and noses. In greeting, we may kiss cheeks repeatedly up to four times, almost as if we are sampling. Kissing the mouth romantically as a part of mate selection is also common in many different cultures but is unnecessary to actual mating. A simple explanation is that the lips and tongue are highly innervated somato-sensorily; hence, we can derive pleasure from the tactile input in a way that parallels romantic couples holding hands, which are also highly innervated. But kissing affords a unique chemosensory opportunity. Kissing is an excellent way to gather myriad types of information on a partner from both volatile and nonvolatile chemicals (Breslin, 2008; Eibl-Eibesfeldt, 1972; Wlodarski & Dunbar, 2013, 2014). A common belief is that "a kiss is the moment when sex and science meet, when we know whether our chemistry matches"(Blue, 2014). Discussions of kissing often lead to a metaphorical pronouncement of two people's simpatico "chemistry," but it is not a metaphor because kissing actually allows their chemistry to be analyzed by the respective senses.

First and foremost, kissing provides information about oral hygiene. And, while this may not be at the forefront of your thoughts during that behavior, if the person you are kissing has poor hygiene, then the first kiss will most likely be the last. A partner who fails in personal hygiene may be a poor choice of partner and future parent. In addition, different bacteria yield different chemical cues, so there is opportunity for evaluating types of oral bacteria present. It is also an opportunity for evaluating salivary and nasopharyngeal mucus compo-nents, which may provide information about genetic status and compatibility. Saliva and mucus compounds carried on breath can also provide information about health, metabolism, and disease. Various cues in sweat and breath can provide information related to immune and inflammatory status (Aksenov et al., 2012; Pijls et al., 2016; Smolinska et al., 2014). There is also evidence that animals can smell internal trauma from another animal's urine (Kimball et al., 2016). Metabolic derangements can also be determined from breath. For exam-ple, people with insulin and blood sugar difficulties are well known to have an acetone odor to their breath (Wang & Wang, 2013). It is also clear that diet affects oral odor and breath, most famously garlic and coffee significantly alter the odor of mouth and breath (Taucher, Hansel, Jordan, & Lindinger, 1996). It might even be possible to identify sexual hormonal status and phase of cycle in women by oral odor (Doty, 1981). And, of course, we may be able to detect gender from oral compounds, as pigs do from androstenone in male saliva. Lewis Thomas is credited with the idea that our HLA genes give us an individualized odor fingerprint that can be used to connote genetic identity and relatedness (Beauchamp & Yamazaki, 1997). These signals are believed to arise from urine and apocrine glands in skin, but they might also be detectable in saliva and in breath (Spielman et al., 1998). The idea that we can both taste and smell nonvolatile and volatile compounds from other people when we kiss them means, strangely, that people have flavor, an integrated signal from taste and smell, that we are able to assess; although this "flavor" may not be one of which we are fully aware. But this idea should not be confused with that of food flavor, as the higher order processing of nutritional chemical and social chemical cues can be separate (Bender et al., 2009; Small et al., 2005; Welge-Lussen et al., 2009).

5.3 General Socializing and Bonding

The proximal chemical senses play an important role in more general human socializing. For example, odors can convey a sense of home, safety, and family that brings an overall sense of ease and comfort. Familiarity with the smell of one's mate, the smell of one's home, the home of a loved one, or the smell of cooking by a parent or grandparent can bring a strong sense of place, comfort, and even belonging (Herz, 2016; see also section 6.2 Taste Is Security). This may be also true of a cuisine in general and the flavor principles associated with it (Rozin, 1973; Weber & Heuberger, 2008). Thus, the smell of cooking from one's childhood may be comforting when ill at ease or in a strange place. Gathering with a group at Grandma's house for her home cooking may create a proximal chemosensory association not only with the "familiar" but moreover with "family." Similarly, gathering socially over food enables social bonds to be built or strengthened. Hence, we are bound to one another over the proverbial "breaking of bread," an act that is also associated with conversation and resource sharing.

In addition to evaluating another person by their conversation, a meal affords an opportunity to evaluate their manners and mores, and their eating behavior itself. These behaviors may include culture-specific habits (using a spoon to aid in putting pasta on a fork or eating with hands), willingness to share food or symmetrical or asymmetrical chewing or chewing with the mouth open or closed. Feeding and socializing also creates the opportunity to learn about the others' recent diet experience via residual olfactory cues. Rodents have been shown to "teach" others about their diet by combining the smell of food on or near them with the smell of relatively invariant pulmonary metabolites on their breath (Galef & Kennett, 1987; Galef & Whiskin, 1997), specifically carbon disulfide signaling (Munger et al., 2010). This experience leads observing animals to prefer to eat the food that the other has eaten, presumably via a social chemical message indicating that this food is safe to eat. Whether such a combinatorial system of food compounds mixed with breath compounds is operational in humans has not been determined.

The family has other dimensions of proximal chemosensory signaling and bonding. For example, infants have been shown to both recognize and prefer the odors of their mothers (on worn shirts) over other recent mothers. And similarly, mothers recognize and prefer the odor of their own infant (on worn clothing) over the odor of other infants' worn clothing (Cernoch & Porter, 1985; Porter, Cernoch, & McLaughlin, 1983). Thus, these studies suggest that in bonding with each other, the mother and the infant come to know the other through their chemical signatures, a phenomenon known to occur in other animals (Broad, Curley, & Keverne, 2006). This leads me to wonder if Harry Harlow's baby monkeys did not also suffer from olfactory deprivation of a nurturer or mother (Harlow, 1958; Harlow & Zimmermann, 1959). In Harlow's famous (or perhaps infamous) studies, he found that infant monkeys reared by an artificial mother made of chicken fence wire with a mask for a face and a milk bottle teat for feeding did not fare nearly as well as baby monkeys reared by a similar artificial mother but one that was covered in a terry cloth towel to simulate fur. The general conclusion was that the somatosensory tactile input of terry cloth was responsible for the relative improvement because it allowed for "emotional attachment" or bonding due to the simulation of cuddling. Whereas there is little doubt that touch is essential for infant development, it is also clear that the terry cloth-wrapped "mother" would have a much more prominent odor than would the chicken wire alone (odors tend to collect on surfaces that have high surface area, such as fur, hair, or cloth). And if more than one monkey used the same surrogate, the terry cloth would have even smelled like another monkey. Thus, we must wonder if there was not also a role of the smell of the cloth in the results that Harlow found in that it provided a more salient stimulus for olfactory bonding with "mother." Others have reported that the inability to smell among newborn mice can prove fatal (Brunet, Gold, & Ngai, 1996), which has been attributed to their inability to find nipples for nursing. The ability to find nipples for nursing in some species is attributed to the secretion of nipple pheromones (Hudson, Labra-Cardero, & Mendoza-Soylovna, 2002; Keverne, 2002; Raihani et al., 2009).

The social ramifications of anosmia raises another social question of the importance of proximal chemosensory cues in socializing and reading others in general. Lemogne et al. found that human anosmics have difficulty interpreting facial cues after their acute loss and must relearn to read social cues to recognize emotions again (Lemogne et al., 2015). This indicates that our ability to smell others when we are near them somehow gates the cortex to understand social cues and expressions. Furthermore, since we argue that facial expressions can cause emotions (See 6.1 The Facial Feedback Hypothesis of Emotion), it is interesting that patients with damage to emotional brain regions, such as the amygdala, have difficulty interpreting facial expressions as well (Adolphs et al., 1994). Thus, social interpretations appear to be linked both to the amygdala and to olfaction via their impact on emotions.

If proximal chemosensory cues are important for human socializing, then there is a problem with modern physical isolation built on the assumption that digital interactions of video, television, and telephone are sufficient. But if they are not sufficient, then feelings of social isolation resulting from lack of chemical cues could lead to heightened feelings of loneliness. Although speculative, Bill Gates has commented that in our current culture, the feeling of isolation and loneliness is the single biggest soluble problem facing society today (Gates, 2017). As an example, if we compare various technological forms of communication, we have general agreement that tweeting and texting is the worst, and emailing is only slightly better. Telephoning is an improvement over email, but most agree that seeing people in a videoconference is better than telephoning. Yet, if a meeting is important – if you want to propose marriage, discuss a diagnosis, or promote or reprimand an employee – we recognize that a personal face-to-face meeting is best. So what information do we receive from a face-to-face meeting that we do not derive from a high-fidelity, high-resolution videoconference in which we can see and hear almost everything. In a videoconference, we cannot touch, taste, or smell the other people. Of course, we also cognitively understand that they are not physically present during a videoconference, but this begs the question, "Why does being physically present matter?" Except perhaps when sharing food, we do not touch or taste people in most meetings, but in any face-to-face meeting, we can smell others. It is curious that we place so much importance on face-to-face meetings over videoconferencing. I will offer the hypothesis that, in terms of the information that passed between individuals in different types of meetings, the main difference is olfactory, and that these physical stimuli and accompanying sensations anchor the meeting as materially real rather than virtual. Thus, one way to overcome loneliness and feelings of isolation might be to physically visit people as much as possible rather than to telephone, videoconference, or FaceTime.

This provides the opportunity for all the senses to be engaged, including the chemical senses. We also know that feelings of loneliness and isolation are enhanced among the elderly, especially within elder-living establishments. Although there are certain to be multiple reasons for this situation, it is also common for elderly people to have a diminished sense of smell (Attems, Walker, & Jellinger, 2015; Cowart, 1989; Wysocki & Gilbert, 1989). I will speculate that a large portion of the heightened sense of isolation sensed by the elderly is due to their chemosensory deficits. Recent evidence has shown that sexual behavior is diminished in older Americans with a poor sense of smell compared to an age-matched sample with a normal sense of smell for their age range (Zhong et al., 2018). The fact that we do not attend to chemical social cues, does not mean they are not there. We experience a form of inattentive blindness to these cues (Lorig, 1999, 2012), but they are present and affecting us.

As an aside, we could also consider that the digitization of material objects, such as books and art, deprives us of their chemosensory cues. Clearly any book that we hold and read will also provide a touch and an odor. The digitization of the world has created a form of chemosensory deprivation, such that we cannot feel, smell, or taste them when they are digitized. For anything that has been digitized – from art, to books, to meetings with other people – has deprived us of all chemosensory inputs, preserving only visual and/or auditory stimulation. Whereas the consequences of this on our health and social lives are unclear, it is certain that we are reducing the richness of our sensory world. If the proximal chemosenses were only a nuisance, this might be acceptable or even preferable, but years of study have shown the enormous and often silent effects of smell and taste on critical features of our lives (Herz, 2008; Lorig, 2012; Zelano et al., 2005). For example, as our chemosensory culture has steadily diminished in recent years, there have been social correlates of this, including less frequent sex (Twenge, Sherman, & Wells, 2017), albeit possibly not causally related.

Summary: Taste and the proximal chemical senses are fundamental drivers of human socializing generally, social feeding, evaluating others, determining compatibility, bonding, mating, and parenting. Their absence due either to sensory loss or stimulus deprivation from digitization of life may be detrimental to our social activities, our ability to function socially and understand one another, and our sense of connectedness to community and family.

6 Emotions

Most, if not all, of the animals on our planet – from fleas to flies and fish to ferrets – are attracted to or repelled by the foods they eat due to flavor. Such approach and avoidance behavior are the *sin qua non* of emotion. While arguing that fleas, flies, and other animals experience emotion is certainly beyond the scope of this document, humans do report conscious feelings of mood, state, and affect that serve both to influence our decisions and to communicate our states to our conspecifics. Although there are many current theories of emotion, my goal here is not to review or summarize them. Rather, I aim to place taste and the proximal chemical senses at the foundational roots of human emotional experience.

Consider the origin of human emotions and the concept of approach and avoidance; it is clear that from the first moments of life, infants are connected to emotion by the chemical senses. While many other sensory and motor systems may orient and direct suckling behavior, flavor leads to its continuance, stoppage, or repulsion (Desor, Maller, & Andrews, 1975; Kare & Beauchamp, 1985; Steiner et al., 2001). This early experience is the foundation for what we later describe as the "pleasures and angsts of our lives." In fact, neonates do not exhibit their emotions beyond crying and being quiescent, as they are too young to spontaneously smile, laugh, show anger, etc.; these develop after a few months of age. Yet, neonates are capable of brainstem reflex facial responses to sweet (lip licking) and bitter tastes (gaping) (Ganchrow, Steiner, & Daher, 1983). Later in life, our emotions may influence our chemosensory preferences. Initially, our emotions may be driven by the brain stem reflexes that trigger licking or gaping, which, in turn, may alter our attitude toward foods and food objects (e.g., mother). It has been demonstrated that a rinse with a bitter solution can alter our mood (Dubovski, Ert, & Niv, 2017) and that, reciprocally, altered mood can influence how we perceive tastes (Noel & Dando, 2015). Evidence from a variety of sources suggest that we are biologically prepared to reject some foods and accept others and that these responses are common in many mammals (Grill & Norgren, 1978a, 1978b; Norgren & Leonard, 1971). The connection of flavor to these ingestion or rejection behaviors is as clear as are the vocalizations and facial expressions associated with them. I have already discussed the nutritional consequences of sugar and dangers of bitter poisons. Children's flavor preferences are largely solidified by the age of four years (Skinner et al., 1999; Skinner et al., 2002). And those experiences shape the individualized expression of bonding, attachment, and emotion (Harlow, 1958). Edmund T. Rolls, in his article on the neurophysiology of emotion, similarly considers flavor acceptance or rejection (approach and avoidance) the origin of emotion and the basis for the neural pathways for the expression of emotion in response to other stimuli (2000).

Among animals, emotional states and their associated body postures, behaviors, facial expressions, and vocalizations are useful in a social communicative sense. Hence, fear and surprise and their associated alarm calls and running for shelter are powerful social messages for the community, "Watch out! Follow my example!" Anger and its associated teeth baring and growling communicate socially, "Whatever you are doing [approaching, invading, attacking, stealing, eating my food, liaising with my mate, etc.], best to stop it, or else!" Happiness and its associated smiling, cooing, purring, relaxed posture may indicate the opposite: "Whatever you are doing [feeding me, grooming me, keeping me warm], keep doing it." Sadness and its associated limp posture, whining, whimpering, crying may indicate, "I am suffering and need your support, assistance, and protection," and so on for other emotions (Parr, Waller, & Fugate, 2005). Yet, neither the expressive behaviors from the exhibitor nor the responses they elicit in observers need be conscious for there to be a social exchange of information.

To wit, we cannot know if ants and flies are conscious, but we can see them communicate socially about resources, invaders, alarm states, and the location of food. These are all clearly indicated through chemical signals that convey a particular message (Blum, 1969). In these species, the social communications cues for their peers are principally chemosensory. Of course, these messages may also be exchanged behaviorally as in the case of bees waggle dancing about food (von Frisch & Lindauer, 1956). Although it is unclear if these animals have emotional states, anyone who has hit a beehive with a stick or kicked an anthill has witnessed what appears to be alarm, surprise, panic, and anger expressed behaviorally by the colony. Anthropomorphizing aside, it is clear that emotions for humans have: (1) an objective behavioral and social component that many other animals possess as well; (2) a subjective conscious state component that only we can know and feel for ourselves but is "intersubjectively confirmable" in our dealings with others in their apparent states; and (3) a strong dependence on our early experience with chemical signals like tastes and smells.

6.1 The Facial Feedback Hypothesis of Emotion

What is the relationship between our emotional actions and our internal subjective emotional states? Is one causal of the other, and if so, in which direction is the causal arrow pointing? Are facial actions an expression of our emotional state (a reaction), or are they the behavioral determinants of emotional state? Or is the influence circular and each influences the other? Can we have "emotional" actions without associated emotional states; i.e., can we express rage behaviorally without feeling rage emotionally? And if so, why do very good actors often retire early claiming the toll their acting took? What happens to our emotions when we force our face to be expressionless; e.g., if we force our face to be blank and relaxed, do our emotions vanish or diminish? Why does laughter therapy (forced laughter and happy facial expressions) have a positive impact on our mood? Is the forced expression of happy motor patterns determining the positive affective and mood response (Strack, Martin, & Stepper, 1988)? Moreover, what does any of this have to do with taste and the proximal chemical senses? I postulate here that appetitive "yum" and avoidance "yuck" facial reflexes of the taste and flavor areas in the brain are the fundamental drivers of positive and negative affective emotional impact in humans.

A theory that facial actions and expressions are both causing and modulating ongoing emotions is over a century and a half old and has garnered a great deal of supporting evidence (Adelmann & Zajonc, 1989). Adelmann and Zajonc (1989) describe the history of this theory beginning with Piderit (1858, 1888) and Gratiolet (1865) who stated that the facial response to the "emotion" of disgust is similar to the facial reflex to tasting aversive taste stimuli (Gratiolet, 1865; Piderit, 1858, 1888). Although Charles Darwin (1872) did not explicitly agree with Piderit and Gratiolet, he admitted the possibility of a causal role of motor efference in the emotional experience. In doing so, he foreshadowed the development of the facial feedback hypothesis (Darwin, 1872). William James went even further to propose that facial expressions are causal to emotional states (1884).

Tomkins (1962) first clearly stated the facial feedback theory of emotions, "the face expresses affect, both to others and to the self, via feedback, which is more rapid and more complex than any stimulation of which the slower moving visceral organs are capable" (pp. 205–206). Tomkins described the facial muscles as more informative of affective state than those of the trunk and extremities, thereby making a clear statement that the face would be the predominant driver of emotion in the feedback theory of emotion. On the minutia of differential facial expressions, Paul Ekman has expounded at great length on the full range of expressions and microexpressions (2003). Experiments in which participants are asked to smile or frown during positive or negative experiences found that people were subjectively more positive affectively when smiling and more negative affectively when frowning (Laird 1974; Rhodewalt & Comer, 1979). Emotions of elation and aggression are manipulated correspondingly by forced smiling or frowning, wherein the voluntary reduction of (or attempts to eliminate) facial reaction reduced emotional experience, in support of what Darwin also observed. Therefore, it seems that the exaggeration of facial efference congruent with an emotional stimulus increases corresponding subjective experience of an emotion, and conversely, inhibition reduces it. And simulating efference incongruent to a stimulus (e.g., forced frowning when happy) also reduces stimulus-consistent subjective experience (Adelmann & Zajonc, 1989). These experiments provide evidence that facial actions can modulate emotional states up and down; further, there are experiments that support a role of facial actions to generate emotions *de novo* (Duncan & Laird, 1977; Rutledge & Hupka, 1985; Strack, Martin, & Stepper, 1988). LeDoux in overall support of this theory claimed that the neuroanatomical connections and processes indicate a powerful role of the sensory process in emotion (1987).

Since taste, from infancy, is a fundamental driver of facial expressions as brainstem reflexes, I suggest that taste as well as flavor are at the root of the positive and negative affect the underlies facial feedback eliciting and modulating emotional states (Steiner, 1973). Taste elicits brainstem facial reflexes determined by the first synaptic relay of the nucleus of the solitary tract (Grill & Norgren, 1978b; Norgren & Leonard, 1971). In humans, appetitive and nutritious stimuli such as sweet-tasting sugars elicit smiling and lip smacking, and aversive stimuli such as the bitter-tasting toxin quinine elicit the drawing down and back of the corners of the mouth (gaping, frowning, and shuddering) (Steiner et al., 2001). Perhaps a corollary perspective is that the brain is a cognitive dissonance emotional engine and is forever interpreting inputs as in, "I am smiling, therefore I must be happy; I am frowning, therefore I must be displeased" – a situation that would have certainly made William James smile.

6.2 Taste Is Security

Given the primordial role of flavor in emotion, it is not far-fetched to consider that flavor (at least good flavors) means security. Emotional security, the sense of feeling safe or being in a safe environment, can be brought about by the notion that we are in a familiar, comforting, or nurturing environment. This can be achieved through food and the odors of cooking via familiar flavors and gastronomy. People in an unfamiliar, frightening, or even threatening environment can be given a sense of comfort by offering them familiar foods and familiar cooking (Rozin, 1973). Although the idea of "home" may not be comforting to everyone, the sense of neighborhood, community, in-group, and culture are supraordinate concepts of familiarity, belonging, and tribe that can make us feel secure. Within this framework, our cultural gastronomy and familiar flavors may be more comforting than our wardrobe, language, or even religion (Dondero & Van Hook, 2016). The feeling of comfort that comes from the familiar tastes and smells of our formative years is an important emotional state that offers a sense of ease and well-being that both uplifts oneself and can be communicated and chemically shared with one's compatriots. A similar emotional state of security can be achieved by being placed into a location that smells of one's home in terms of either building, earth, or neighborhood odors. And should one smell the odor, clothing, perfume, etc. of a loved one, this too may be able to make one feel a sense of comfort and security.

Summary: Emotions have their origin in infantile responses to flavor and can be helpful when they assist in decisions that must be made quickly and allow one to communicate affective (good and bad) concerns and beliefs with others, such as "we are under attack" or "we are safe." One theory of emotion is based on the idea that feedback from facial muscles, skin, and or vasculature (the facial efference theory of emotion) induces associated feelings in the mind. That is, facial actions and expressions cause feelings of emotion. The primordial facial reflexes of smiling and frowning are bound to brainstem neurocircuitry that controls responses to taste stimuli such as sugars (sweet) and toxins (bitter). Thus, I hypothesize that taste and flavor are primordial drivers of basic affective states and emotions and that the tastes, odors, and flavors of our formative years can bring a sense of comfort and security.

7 Summary

The question "**Are You Going To Eat That?**", which serves as the subtitle of this Element, touches on the continuously updated understanding of past, present, and future encompassed in a single phenomenon that represents the proximal chemosensory intersection of social gathering, interpersonal interaction, bonding, feeding, and nutrition. The question is dynamic and implicates both the nutritional and the social in this chemosensory context. It is a fine example of how the proximal chemical senses provide a means for interacting and understanding the people, the food, and the basic biological pillars of social network, nutrition, and reproduction.

Glossary

Chemesthesis: This term is the contraction of the words "chemical" and "somesthesis." It represents the sense of chemicals on epidermis and epithelia and can elicit most skin sensations, including warm, cool, hot, cold, touch, vibration, pain, sting, irritation, and others. Examples are the burn of chili peppers from the compound capsaicin and the cool of mint from the compound menthol.

Chemical Senses: The chemical senses encompass all sensory experience from chemicals acting on our bodies. Traditionally, these are described as the senses of olfaction, gustation, and chemesthesis. There are other aspects of chemical senses that go beyond these three sensory modalities, such as the activation of the vomeronasal organ by semiochemicals, but smell, taste, and the skin senses are the biggest three modalities within the chemical senses.

Chemical Somesthesis: This is synonymous with chemesthesis.

Chemosensory: The sensory systems that subserve the chemical senses. Chemosensory stimuli are those compounds or chemicals that act on these sensory systems.

Engram: A mental image or memory of how we expect a stimulus to be perceived. It allows us to determine during a stimulus experience if it appears as expected. For example, it is the basis for comparing sampled food with our expectation for that food that allows to know when a food has spoiled.

Enteroceptors: This is an overarching term to refer to the groupings of internal receptors that allow one's physiology to monitor what compounds (particularly nutrients) are in body fluids, especially blood and cerebrospinal fluid.

Epidermis: This is the covering of the body, otherwise known as our skin. It is the largest organ of the body and is a chemosensory organ.

Epithelium: This is the covering inside the openings of our body. It is like epidermis but is typically red or pink in appearance, is thinner, and lacks a heavy cornified layer of dead cells on the top. The body openings that are lined with epithelium include: the mouth (including gums and tongue) and throat (and the entire gastrointestinal tract); the nostrils and inside the nose; around the eyes; under the eyelids; the rectum; the vagina; and the urethra. All of these epithelia are chemosensory surfaces.

Exteroceptors: This is an overarching term to refer to the groupings of external receptors that allow one's physiology to monitor what compounds (particularly nutrients) are about to be swallowed, have entered the gastro-intestinal tract, and will be absorbed.

Flehmen Response: The Flehmen response or reaction is the curling back of the upper lip and exposing teeth, usually associated with contact with semiotic compounds or fluids, such as urine. The behavior is thought to facilitate the transport of social compounds to the vomeronasal organ located in the roof of the mouth or the nasal septum, depending on species. The behavior is most commonly seen in horses, antelopes, cats, and related species.

Gedanken: This is a German term used by scientists to indicate a mental manipulation or the exercise of a "thought" experiment, as in, "As a *gedanken* experiment, I wondered whether human infertility would decrease if people all stopped using soaps, deodorants, and perfumes."

Gustation: This is the formal term to refer to the sense of taste or related to the sense of taste. Also, gustatory.

Motor Efference: This term refers to the neural signals that contract muscles and sense when muscles have contracted sending a signal to the brain that these muscles have contracted and by how much. It is in effect a neural reflection of what the muscles are doing.

Nasopharynx: This refers to the region of epithelium at the back of the throat that is above the level of the mouth and lies between the back of the nose and the throat.

Olfaction: This is the formal term to refer to the sense of smell or related to the sense of smell. Also, olfactory.

Papillae: This term refers to the small bumps and folds on the tongue that make it rough. They include the filiform, the fungiform, the foliate, and the circumvallate papillae. All but the filiform papillae can contain taste buds.

Sapid: This refers to compounds that can elicit a taste or affect taste buds. Sapid molecules are ones that we can taste, although strictly speaking, this refers to positive tastes.

Semiochemicals: A social chemical given from one animal to another, such as a pheromone, to influence the other animal's behavior, mood, or physiological processes.

Sensory Modality: A sensory modality is a major sensory system defined by both the peripheral sensory organs and the sensory experiences generated from activation of these organs. The five main sensory modalities are: taste, smell, somesthesis, vision, and hearing. Modalities are supraordinate to qualities, which are subdivisions of experience within a modality, such as sweet, sour, floral, musty, hot, cold, red, blue, C-sharp, and G-flat.

Somesthesis: This is a sensory modality that refers to the senses of the body. More commonly, the term is used to refer to the skin senses and their associated sensations of touch, pressure, vibration, stretch, cool, warm, hot, cold, pain, tickle, itch, sting, numbing, prickling, burning, etc.

Taste Pore: A taste pore is the opening or hole in the oral epithelium by which each taste bud gains access to the fluids, solutions, and juices that enter the oral cavity. Without a taste pore, a taste bud would have no access to any of the stimuli within the oral cavity, since the taste bud is embedded within the oral epithelium, and consequently, there could be no taste.

Volatile: This is a chemistry term used to refer to a molecule's ability to be a gas or enter the vapor phase from a solution or liquid phase. Most molecules that we smell are volatile. The approximate weight threshold for a molecule to become volatile is less than 300 Daltons. Molecules must also be able to separate from their solvents or substrates to become volatile.

Vomeronasal Organ: The vomeronasal organ is one of the sensory systems that serve social chemical communication. It is thought that most phero- mones act either via the main olfactory system or via the vomeronasal system. It can respond to both volatile and nonvolatile compounds (e.g., the Flehmen response). The organ is a pit or cul-de-sac in either the oral palate or the nasal septum, depending upon the species. It contains two unique classes of receptors and can influence an animal's mood, behavior, or modulate physiology. Humans have a vomeronasal organ in the nasal septum, but it appears to be vestigial.

References

Adelmann, P. K., & Zajonc, R. B. (1989). Facial efference and the experience of emotion. *Annual Review of Psychology, 40*, 249–280.

Adolphs, R., Tranel, D., Damasio, H., & Damasio, A. (1994). Impaired recognition of emotion in facial expressions following bilateral damage to the human amygdala. *Nature, 372*(6507), 669–672. doi:10.1038/372669a0

Aksenov, A. A., Gojova, A., Zhao, W., Morgan, J. T., Sankaran, S., Sandrock, C. E., & Davis, C. E. (2012). Characterization of volatile organic compounds in human leukocyte antigen heterologous expression systems: a cell's "chemical odor fingerprint". *Chembiochem, 13*(7), 1053–1059. doi:10.1002/cbic.201200011

Allen, M. L., Yovovich, V., & Wilmers, C. C. (2016). Evaluating the responses of a territorial solitary carnivore to potential mates and competitors. *Sci Rep, 6*, 27257. doi:10.1038/srep27257

Attems, J., Walker, L., & Jellinger, K. A. (2015). Olfaction and aging: A mini-review. *Gerontology, 61*(6), 485–490. doi:10.1159/000381619

Bartelt, R. J., Schaner, A. M., & Jackson, L. L. (1985). cis-Vaccenyl acetate as an aggregation pheromone in Drosophila melanogaster. *J Chem Ecol, 11*(12), 1747–1756. doi:10.1007/BF01012124

Beauchamp, G. K., & Yamazaki, K. (1997). HLA and mate selection in humans: commentary. *Am J Hum Genet, 61*(3), 494–496. doi:10.1086/515521

Behrens, M., & Meyerhof, W. (2010). Oral and extraoral bitter taste receptors. *Results Probl Cell Differ, 52*, 87–99. doi:10.1007/978-3-642-14426-4_8

Bender, G., Hummel, T., Negoias, S., & Small, D. M. (2009). Separate signals for orthonasal vs. retronasal perception of food but not nonfood odors. *Behav Neurosci, 123*(3), 481–489. doi:10.1037/a0015065

Berthoud, H. R. (2002). Multiple neural systems controlling food intake and body weight. *Neurosci Biobehav Rev, 26*(4), 393–428.

Besnard, P., Passilly-Degrace, P., & Khan, N. A. (2016). Taste of fat: A sixth taste modality? *Physiol Rev, 96*(1), 151–176. doi:10.1152/physrev.00002.2015

Billeter, J. C., Atallah, J., Krupp, J. J., Millar, J. G., & Levine, J. D. (2009). Specialized cells tag sexual and species identity in Drosophila melanogaster. *Nature, 461*(7266), 987–991. doi:10.1038/nature08495

Birch, L. L., McPhee, L., Steinberg, L., & Sullivan, S. (1990). Conditioned flavor preferences in young children. *Physiol Behav, 47*(3), 501–505.

Bowman, E., & Tatar, M. (2016). Reproduction regulates Drosophila nutrient intake through independent effects of egg production and sex peptide:

Implications for aging. *Nutr Healthy Aging*, 4(1), 55–61. doi:10.3233/NHA-1613.

Blue, V. (2014). *Kissing: A Field Guide*. Berkeley, CA: Cleis Press Inc.

Blum, M. S. (1969). Alarm pheromones. *Annual Review of Entomology*, *14*, 57–80.

Breslin, P., & Huang, L. (2006). Human Taste: Peripheral Anatomy, Taste Transduction, and Coding. In T. Hummel & A. Welge-Lüssen (Eds.), *Taste and Smell: An Update* (Vol. 63, pp. 152–190). Basel: Karger.

Breslin, P. A. (2013). An evolutionary perspective on food and human taste. *Curr Biol*, *23*(9), R409–418. doi:10.1016/j.cub.2013.04.010

Breslin, P. A., Beauchamp, G. K., & Pugh, E. N. J. (1996). Monogeusia for fructose, glucose, sucrose, and maltose. *Perception and Psychophysics*, *58*(3), 327–341.

Breslin, P. A., & Spector, A. C. (2008).Mammalian taste perception. *Curr Biol*, *18*(4), R148–155. doi:10.1016/j.cub.2007.12.017

Breslin, P. A. S. (2008). Multi-modal sensory integration: Evaluating foods and mates. *Chemosensory Perception*, *1*, 92–94.

Breslin, P. A. S. (2018). The Sense of Taste Encompasses Two Roles: Conscious Taste Perception and Subconscious Metabolic Responses. In D. J. Linden (Ed.), *Think Tank: Forty Neuroscientists Explore the Biological Roots of Human Experience* (pp. 110–118). New Haven: Yale University Press.

Breslin, P.A.S., Gilmore, M.M., Beauchamp, G.K., & Green, B.G. (1993). Psychophysical evidence that oral astringency is a tactile sensation. *Chemical Senses*, 18(4), 405–417. https://doi.org/10.1093/chemse/18.4.405

Broad, K. D., Curley, J. P., & Keverne, E. B. (2006). Mother-infant bonding and the evolution of mammalian social relationships. *Philos Trans R Soc Lond B Biol Sci*, *361*(1476), 2199–2214. doi:10.1098/rstb.2006.1940

Brunet, L. J., Gold, G. H., & Ngai, J. (1996). General anosmia caused by a targeted disruption of the mouse olfactory cyclic nucleotide-gated cation channel. *Neuron*, *17*(4), 681–693.

Buchinger, T. J., Li, W., & Johnson, N. S. (2014). Bile salts as semiochemicals in fish. *Chem Senses*, *39*(8), 647–654. doi:10.1093/chemse/bju039

Cain, W. S., de Wijk, R., Lulejian, C., Schiet, F., & See, L. C. (1998). Odor identification: perceptual and semantic dimensions. *Chem Senses*, *23*(3), 309–326.

Caprio, J., Brand, J. G., Teeter, J. H., Valentincic, T., Kalinoski, D. L., Kohbara, J., . . . Wegert, S. (1993). The taste system of the channel catfish: from biophysics to behavior. *Trends Neurosci*, *16*(5), 192–197.

Cernoch, J. M., & Porter, R. H. (1985). Recognition of maternal axillary odors by infants. *Child Dev*, *56*(6), 1593–1598.

Chaudhari, N., & Roper, S. D. (2010). The cell biology of taste. *J Cell Biol*, *190*(3), 285–296. doi:10.1083/jcb.201003144

Chen, Q. Y., Alarcon, S., Tharp, A., Ahmed, O. M., Estrella, N. L., Greene, T. A., . . . Breslin, P. A. (2009). Perceptual variation in umami taste and polymorphisms in TAS1 R taste receptor genes. *American Journal of Clinical Nutrition*, *90*(3), 770S–779S. doi:10.3945/ajcn.2009.27462 N

Chen, S., Lee, A. Y., Bowens, N. M., Huber, R., & Kravitz, E. A. (2002). Fighting fruit flies: A model system for the study of aggression. *Proc Natl Acad Sci USA*, *99*(8), 5664–5668. doi:10.1073/pnas.082102599

Cowart, B. J. (1989). Relationships between taste and smell across the adult life span. *Ann N Y Acad Sci*, *561*, 39–55.

Cox, C. R., & Le Boeuf, B. J. (1977). Female incitation of male competition: A mechanism in sexual selection. *American Naturalist*, *111*, 317–335.

Darwin, C. (1872). *The Expression of the Emotions in Man and Animals*. London: John Murray.

Depoortere, I. (2014). Taste receptors of the gut: emerging roles in health and disease. *Gut*, *63*(1), 179–190. doi:10.1136/gutjnl-2013-305112

Desor, J. A., Maller, O., & Andrews, K. (1975). Ingestive responses of human newborns to salty, sour, and bitter stimuli. *J Comp Physiol Psychol*, *89*(8), 966–970.

Dondero, M., & Van Hook, J. (2016). Generational status, neighborhood context, and mother-child resemblance in dietary quality in Mexican-origin families. *Social Science & Medicine*, *150*, 212–220.

Doty, R. L. (1981). Olfactory communication in humans. *Chemical Senses*, *6*, 351–376.

Dubovski, N., Ert, E., & Niv, M. (2017). Bitter mouth-rinse affects emotions. *Food Quality and Preference*, 60, 154–164. doi:10.1016/j.foodqual.2017.04.007

Dudley, R. (2014). *The Drunken Monkey: Why We Drink and Abuse Alcohol*. Oakland: University of California Press.

Duncan, J. L., & Laird, J. D. (1977). Cross-modality consistencies in individual differences in self-attribution. *Journal of Personality*, *45*, 191–206.

Eibl-Eibesfeldt, I. (1972). *Love and Hate: The Natural History of Behavior Patterns*. Austin: Holt, Rinehart and Winston.

Ekman, P. (2003). *Emotions Revealed: Recognizing Faces and Feelings to Improve Communication and Emotional Life*. New York: Henry Holt.

Enns, J. T., & Rensink, R. A. (1990). Influence of scene-based properties on visual search. *Science*, *247*(4943), 721–723.

Fan, P., Manoli, D. S., Ahmed, O. M., Chen, Y., Agarwal, N., Kwong, S., . . . Shah, N. M. (2013). Genetic and neural mechanisms that inhibit Drosophila from mating with other species. *Cell*, *154*(1), 89–102. doi:10.1016/j.cell.2013.06.008

Finger, T. E., Bottger, B., Hansen, A., Anderson, K. T., Alimohammadi, H., & Silver, W. L. (2003). Solitary chemoreceptor cells in the nasal cavity serve as sentinels of respiration. *Proc Natl Acad Sci U S A*, *100*(15), 8981–8986. doi:10.1073/pnas.1531172100

Galef, B. G., Jr., & Kennett, D. J. (1987). Different mechanisms for social transmission of diet preference in rat pups of different ages. *Dev Psychobiol*, *20*(2), 209–215. doi:10.1002/dev.420200209

Galef, B. G., Jr., & Whiskin, E. E. (1997). Effects of social and asocial learning on longevity of food-preference traditions. *Anim Behav*, *53*(6), 1313–1322.

Ganchrow, J. R., Steiner, J. E., & Daher, M. (1983). Neonatal facial expressions in response to different qualities and intensities of gustatory stimuli. *Infant Behavior & Development*, 6(4), 473–484. http://dx.doi.org/10.1016/S0163-6383(83)90301-6

Garcia, J., Hankins, W. G., & Rusiniak, K. W. (1976). Letter: Flavor aversion studies. *Science*, *192*(4236), 265–267.

Garcia, J., Lasiter, P. S., Bermudez-Rattoni, F., & Deems, D. A. (1985). A general theory of aversion learning. *Ann N Y Acad Sci*, *443*, 8–21.

Gates, W. (2017). Bill Gates has humble expectations for the biggest issue tech can solve in the next 10 years. *Quartz*, February 27, 2017. https://qz.com /920314/bill-gates-thinks-isolation-is-the-most-pressing-problem-technology-can-solve-within-the-next-10-years/

Giacometti, T. (1979). Free and bound glutamate in natural products. In L. J. J. Filer (Ed.), *Glutamic Acid: Advances in Biochemistry and Physiology* (pp. 25–34). New York: Raven Press.

Glendinning, J. I., Tarre, M., & Asaoka, K. (1999). Contribution of different bitter-sensitive taste cells to feeding inhibition in a caterpillar (Manduca sexta). *Behav Neurosci*, *113*(4), 840–854.

Grammer, K., Fink, B., & Neave, N. (2005). Human pheromones and sexual attraction. *Eur J Obstet Gynecol Reprod Biol*, *118*(2), 135–142. doi:10.1016/j.ejogrb.2004.08.010

Gratiolet, P. (1865). *De la physionomie et des mouvements d' expression*. Paris: Hetzel.

Green, B.G. (1993). Oral astringency: a tactile component of flavor. *Acta Psychol (Amst)*, 84(1),119–125. PMID: 8237452

Greenspan, R. J., & Ferveur, J. F. (2000). Courtship in Drosophila. *Annu Rev Genet*, *34*, 205–232. doi:10.1146/annurev.genet.34.1.205

Grill, H. J., & Norgren, R. (1978a). The taste reactivity test. I. Mimetic responses to gustatory stimuli in neurologically normal rats. *Brain Res*, *143*(2), 263–279.

Grill, H. J., & Norgren, R. (1978b). The taste reactivity test. II. Mimetic responses to gustatory stimuli in chronic thalamic and chronic decerebrate rats. *Brain Res*, *143*(2), 281–297.

Gurkan, S., & Bradley, R. M. (1987). Autonomic control of von Ebner's lingual salivary glands and implications for taste sensation. *Brain Res*, *419*(1–2), 287–293.

Harlow, H. F. (1958). The nature of love. *American Psychologist*, *13*, 673–685.

Harlow, H. F., & Zimmermann, R. R. (1959). Affectional responses in the infant monkey. *Science*, *130*, 421–432.

Havlicek, J., & Roberts, S. C. (2009). MHC-correlated mate choice in humans: a review. *Psychoneuroendocrinology*, *34*(4), 497–512. doi:10.1016/j.psyneuen.2008.10.007

Haxby, J. V., Hoffman, E. A., & Gobbini, M. I. (2000). The distributed human neural system for face perception. *Trends Cogn Sci*, *4*(6), 223–233.

Herness, S., Zhao, F. L., Kaya, N., Shen, T., Lu, S. G., & Cao, Y. (2005). Communication routes within the taste bud by neurotransmitters and neuropeptides. *Chem Senses*, *30 Suppl 1*, i37–38. doi:10.1093/chemse/bjh101

Herz, R. (2008). *The Scent of Desire: Discovering Our Enigmatic Sense of Smell*. New York: Harper Perennial.

Herz, R. S. (2016). The role of odor-evoked memory in psychological and physiological health. *Brain Sci*, *6*(3). doi:10.3390/brainsci6030022

Howitt, M. R., Lavoie, S., Michaud, M., Blum, A. M., Tran, S. V., Weinstock, J. V., . . . Garrett, W. S. (2016). Tuft cells, taste-chemosensory cells, orchestrate parasite type 2 immunity in the gut. *Science*, *351*(6279), 1329–1333. doi:10.1126/science.aaf1648

Hudson, R., Labra-Cardero, D., & Mendoza-Soylovna, A. (2002). Sucking, not milk, is important for the rapid learning of nipple-search odors in newborn rabbits. *Dev Psychobiol*, *41*(3), 226–235. doi:10.1002/dev.10073

Jacob, S., McClintock, M. K., Zelano, B., & Ober, C. (2002). Paternally inherited HLA alleles are associated with women's choice of male odor. *Nat Genet*, *30*(2), 175–179. doi:10.1038/ng830

Jaeggi, A. V., & Gurven, M. (2013). Natural Cooperators: Food Sharing in Humans and Other Primates. *Evolutionary Anthropology*, *22*, 186–195.

James, W. (1884). What is an emotion? *Mind*, *9*, 188–205.

Janetos, A. C. (1980). Strategies of female mate choice: A theoretical analysis. *Behavioral Ecology and Sociobiology*, *7*, 107–112.

Jiang, P., Josue, J., Li, X., Glaser, D., Li, W., Brand, J. G., . . . Beauchamp, G. K. (2012). Major taste loss in carnivorous mammals. *Proc Natl Acad Sci U S A*, *109*(13), 4956–4961. doi:10.1073/pnas.1118360109

Kare, M. R., & Beauchamp, G. K. (1985). The role of taste in the infant diet. *American Journal of Clinical Nutrition, 41*(2 Suppl), 418–422. doi:10.1093/ajcn/41.2.418

Kass, M. D., Rosenthal, M. C., Pottackal, J., & McGann, J. P. (2013). Fear learning enhances neural responses to threat-predictive sensory stimuli. *Science, 342*(6164), 1389–1392. doi:10.1126/science.1244916

Katz, S. E. (2012). *The Art of Fermentation: An In-Depth Exploration of Essential Concepts and Processes from around the World*. White River Junction: Chelsea Green Publishing.

Keverne, E. B. (1999). The vomeronasal organ. *Science, 286*(5440), 716–720.

Keverne, E. B. (2002). Pheromones, vomeronasal function, and gender-specific behavior. *Cell, 108*(6), 735–738.

Kim, U., Wooding, S., Ricci, D., Jorde, L. B., & Drayna, D. (2005). Worldwide haplotype diversity and coding sequence variation at human bitter taste receptor loci. *Hum Mutat, 26*(3), 199–204. doi:10.1002/humu.20203

Kim, U. K., Breslin, P. A. S., Reed, D., & Drayna, D. (2004). Genetics of Human Taste Perception. *Journal of Dental Research, 83*(6), 448–453.

Kimball, B. A., Cohen, A. S., Gordon, A. R., Opiekun, M., Martin, T., Elkind, J., ... Beauchamp, G. K. (2016). Brain injury alters volatile metabolome. *Chem Senses, 41*(5), 407–414. doi:10.1093/chemse/bjw014

Kinnamon, S. C. (1988). Taste transduction: a diversity of mechanisms. *Trends Neurosci, 11*(11), 491–496.

Kromer, J., Hummel, T., Pietrowski, D., Giani, A. S., Sauter, J., Ehninger, G., ... Croy, I. (2016). Influence of HLA on human partnership and sexual satisfaction. *Sci Rep, 6*, 32550. doi:10.1038/srep32550

Laird, J. D. (1974). Self-attribution of emotion: The effects of expressive behavior on the quality of emotional experience. *Journal of Personality and Social Psychology, 29*, 475–486.

Lapis, T. J., Penner, M. H., Balto, A. S., & Lim, J. (2017). Oral digestion and perception of starch: Effects of cooking, tasting time, and salivary alpha-amylase activity. *Chem Senses, 42*(8), 635–645. doi:10.1093/chemse/bjx042

Lawless, H.T., Schlake, S., Smythe, J., Lim, J., Yang, H., Chapman, K., & Bolton, B. (2004). Metallic taste and retronasal smell. *Chem Senses, 29*(1), 25–33. PMID: 14752037

LeDoux, J. E. (1987). Emotion. In F. Plum (Ed.), *Handbook of Physiology: The Nervous System* (pp. 419–459). Washington, DC: American Physiological Society.

Lee, S. J., Depoortere, I., & Hatt, H. (2018). Therapeutic potential of ectopic olfactory and taste receptors. *Nat Rev Drug Discov*. doi:10.1038/s41573-018-0002-3

Lemogne, C., Smadja, J., Zerdazi el, H., Soudry, Y., Robin, M., Berthoz, S., . . . Bonfils, P. (2015). Congenital anosmia and emotion recognition: A case-control study. *Neuropsychologia*, *72*, 52–58. doi:10.1016/j. neuropsychologia.2015.04.028

Lenfestey, M. W., & Neu, J. (2017). Probiotics in newborns and children. *Pediatr Clin North Am*, *64*(6), 1271–1289. doi:10.1016/j.pcl.2017.08.006

Li, X. (2009). T1 R receptors mediate mammalian sweet and umami taste. *American Journal of Clinical Nutrition*, *90*(3), 733S–737S. doi:10.3945/ ajcn.2009.27462 G

Li, X., Li, W., Wang, H., Cao, J., Maehashi, K., Huang, L., . . . Brand, J. G. (2005). Pseudogenization of a sweet-receptor gene accounts for cats' indifference toward sugar. *PLoS Genet*, *1*(1), 27–35. doi:10.1371/journal. pgen.0010003

Li, X., Staszewski, L., Xu, H., Durick, K., Zoller, M., & Adler, E. (2002). Human receptors for sweet and umami taste. *Proc Natl Acad Sci*, *99*, 4692–4696.

Lorig, T. S. (1999). On the similarity of odor and language perception. *Neurosci Biobehav Rev*, *23*(3), 391–398.

Lorig, T. S. (2012). Beyond self-report: Brain imaging at the threshold of odor perception. *Chemosensory Perception*, *5*, 46–54.

Maddigan, S. L., Feeny, D. H., & Johnson, J. A. (2005). Health-related quality of life deficits associated with diabetes and comorbidities in a Canadian National Population Health Survey. *Qual Life Res*, *14*(5), 1311–1320.

Mandel, A. L., & Breslin, P. A. (2012). High endogenous salivary amylase activity is associated with improved glycemic homeostasis following starch ingestion in adults. *J Nutr*, *142*(5), 853–858. doi:10.3945/jn.111.156984

Mattes, R. D. (1994). Influences on acceptance of bitter foods and beverages. *Physiol Behav*, *56*(6), 1229–1236.

Mattes, R. D. (1997). The taste for salt in humans. *American Journal of Clinical Nutrition*, *65*(2), 692S–697S.

McBurney, D. H., & Gent, J. F. (1979). On the nature of taste qualities. *Psychol Bull*, *86*(1), 151–167.

McGann, J. P. (2013). Presynaptic inhibition of olfactory sensory neurons: New mechanisms and potential functions. *Chem Senses*, *38*(6), 459–474. doi:10.1093/chemse/bjt018

Meredith, M. (2001). Human vomeronasal organ function: a critical review of best and worst cases. *Chem Senses*, *26*(4), 433–445.

Munger, S. D., Leinders-Zufall, T., McDougall, L. M., Cockerham, R. E., Schmid, A., Wandernoth, P., . . . Kelliher, K. R. (2010). An olfactory subsystem that detects carbon disulfide and mediates food-related social learning. *Curr Biol*, *20*(16), 1438–1444. doi:10.1016/j.cub.2010.06.021

Murphy, C., Cardello, A. V., & Brand, J. (1981). Tastes of fifteen halide salts following water and NaCl: Anion and cation effects. *Physiol Behav, 26*(6), 1083–1095.

Nissim, I., Dagan-Wiener, A., & Niv, M. Y. (2017). The taste of toxicity: A quantitative analysis of bitter and toxic molecules. *IUBMB Life, 69*(12), 938–946. doi:10.1002/iub.1694

Noel, C., Dando, R. (2015). The effect of emotional state on taste perception. *Appetite, 95*, 89–95. doi:10.1016/j.appet.2015.06.003

Norgren, R., & Leonard, C. M. (1971). Taste pathways in rat brainstem. *Science, 173*(4002), 1136–1139.

Papes, F., Logan, D. W., & Stowers, L. (2010). The vomeronasal organ mediates interspecies defensive behaviors through detection of protein pheromone homologs. *Cell, 141*(4), 692–703. doi:10.1016/j.cell.2010.03.037

Parr, L. A., Waller, B. M., & Fugate, J. (2005). Emotional communication in primates: implications for neurobiology. *Curr Opin Neurobiol, 15*(6), 716–720. doi:10.1016/j.conb.2005.10.017

Peyrot des Gachons, C., Beauchamp, G. K., Stern, R. M., Koch, K. L., & Breslin, P. A. (2011). Bitter taste induces nausea. *Curr Biol, 21*(7), R247–248. doi:10.1016/j.cub.2011.02.028

Piderit, T. (1858). *Grundzuge der Mimik und Physiognomik.* Braunschweig: Vieweg und Sohn.

Piderit, T. (1888). *La Mimique et la physiognomie.* Paris: Alcan.

Pijls, K. E., Smolinska, A., Jonkers, D. M., Dallinga, J. W., Masclee, A. A., Koek, G. H., & van Schooten, F. J. (2016). A profile of volatile organic compounds in exhaled air as a potential non-invasive biomarker for liver cirrhosis. *Sci Rep, 6*, 19903. doi:10.1038/srep19903

Porter, R. H., Cernoch, J. M., & McLaughlin, F. J. (1983). Maternal recognition of neonates through olfactory cues. *Physiol Behav, 30*(1), 151–154.

Powley, T. L., & Berthoud, H. R. (1985). Diet and cephalic phase insulin responses. *American Journal of Clinical Nutrition, 42*(5 Suppl), 991–1002. doi:10.1093/ajcn/42.5.991

Quinn, W. G., & Greenspan, R. J. (1984). Learning and courtship in Drosophila: Two stories with mutants. *Annu Rev Neurosci, 7*, 67–93. doi:10.1146/annurev.ne.07.030184.000435

Raihani, G., Gonzalez, D., Arteaga, L., & Hudson, R. (2009). Olfactory guidance of nipple attachment and suckling in kittens of the domestic cat: Inborn and learned responses. *Dev Psychobiol, 51*(8), 662–671. doi:10.1002/dev.20401

Rhodewalt, F., & Comer, R. (1979). Induced compliance attitude change: once more with feeling. *Journal of Experimental Social Psychology, 15*, 35–47.

Rolls, E. T. (2000). Precis of the brain and emotion. *Behav Brain Sci, 23*(2), 177–191; discussion 192–233.

Rozin, E. (1973). *The Flavor-Principle Cookbook.* Portland: Hawthorn Books.

Running, C. A., Craig, B. A., & Mattes, R. D. (2015). Oleogustus: The unique taste of fat. *Chem Senses, 40*(7), 507–516. doi:10.1093/chemse/bjv036

Rutledge, L. L., & Hupka, R. B. (1985). The facial feedback hypothesis: Methodological concerns and new supporting evidence. *Motivation and Emotion, 9,* 219–240.

Sandell, M. A., & Breslin, P. A. (2006). Variability in a taste-receptor gene determines whether we taste toxins in food. *Curr Biol, 16*(18), R792–794. doi:10.1016/j.cub.2006.08.049

Sato, K., Endo, S., & Tomita, H. (2002). Sensitivity of three loci on the tongue and soft palate to four basic tastes in smokers and non-smokers. *Acta Otolaryngol Suppl, 546,* 74–82.

Scalera, G. (2002). Effects of conditioned food aversions on nutritional behavior in humans. *Nutr Neurosci, 5*(3), 159–188. doi:10.1080/10284150290013059

Schiffman, S. S., & Dackis, C. (1975). Taste of nutrients: Amino acids, vitamins, and fatty acids. *Perception & Psychophysics, 17,* 140–146.

Sclafani, A., & Nissenbaum, J. W. (1988). Robust conditioned flavor preference produced by intragastric starch infusions in rats. *Am J Physiol, 255*(4 Pt 2), R672–675. doi: 10.1152/ajpregu.1988.255.4.R672

Siniscalchi, M., d'Ingeo, S., Minunno, M., & Quaranta, A. (2018). Communication in dogs. *Animals (Basel), 8*(8). doi:10.3390/ani8080131

Skinner, J. D., Carruth, B. R., Houck, K. S., Bounds, W., Morris, M., Cox, D. R., . . . Coletta, F. (1999). Longitudinal study of nutrient and food intakes of white preschool children aged 24 to 60 months. *J Am Diet Assoc, 99*(12), 1514–1521. doi:10.1016/S0002-8223(99)00371-5

Skinner, J. D., Carruth, B. R., Wendy, B., & Ziegler, P. J. (2002). Children's food preferences: a longitudinal analysis. *J Am Diet Assoc, 102*(11), 1638–1647.

Small, D. M., Gerber, J. C., Mak, Y. E., & Hummel, T. (2005). Differential neural responses evoked by orthonasal versus retronasal odorant perception in humans. *Neuron, 47*(4), 593–605. doi:10.1016/j.neuron.2005.07.022

Smolinska, A., Klaassen, E. M., Dallinga, J. W., van de Kant, K. D., Jobsis, Q., Moonen, E. J., . . . van Schooten, F. J. (2014). Profiling of volatile organic compounds in exhaled breath as a strategy to find early predictive signatures of asthma in children. *PLoS One, 9*(4), e95668. doi:10.1371/journal.pone.0095668

Spielman, A. I., Sunavala, G., Harmony, J. A., Stuart, W. D., Leyden, J. J., Turner, G., . . . Preti, G. (1998). Identification and immunohistochemical localization of protein precursors to human axillary odors in apocrine glands and secretions. *Arch Dermatol, 134*(7), 813–818.

Steiner, J. E. (1973). The gustofacial response: Observation on normal and anencephalic newborn infants. *Symp Oral Sens Percept, 4,* 254–278.

Steiner, J. E., Glaser, D., Hawilo, M. E., & Berridge, K. C. (2001). Comparative expression of hedonic impact: affective reactions to taste by human infants and other primates. *Neurosci Biobehav Rev, 25*(1), 53–74.

Stern, K., & McClintock, M. K. (1998). Regulation of ovulation by human pheromones. *Nature, 392*(6672), 177–179. doi:10.1038/32408

Sternini, C., Anselmi, L., & Rozengurt, E. (2008). Enteroendocrine cells: a site of "taste" in gastrointestinal chemosensing. *Curr Opin Endocrinol Diabetes Obes, 15*(1), 73–78. doi:10.1097/MED.0b013e3282f43a73

Stillman, J. A. (1993). Color influences flavor identification in fruit-flavored beverages. *Journal of Food Science, 58,* 810–812.

Stoddart, D. M. (1990). *Scented Ape: Biology of Human Odour.* Cambridge: Cambridge University Press.

Strack, F., Martin, L. L., & Stepper, S. (1988). Inhibiting and facilitating conditions of the human smile: A nonobtrusive test of the facial feedback hypothesis. *J Pers Soc Psychol, 54*(5), 768–777.

Sun, J., & Chang, E. B. (2014). Exploring gut microbes in human health and disease: Pushing the envelope. *Genes Dis, 1*(2), 132–139. doi:10.1016/j.gendis.2014.08.001

Taucher, J., Hansel, A., Jordan, A., & Lindinger, W. (1996). Analysis of compounds in human breath after ingestion of garlic using proton-transfer-reaction mass spectrometry. *Journal of Agricultural and Food Chemistry, 44,* 3778–3782.

Taylor, A. J. (1996). Volatile flavor release from foods during eating. *Crit Rev Food Sci Nutr, 36*(8), 765–784. doi:10.1080/10408399609527749

Teff, K. L., Devine, J., & Engelman, K. (1995). Sweet taste: Effect on cephalic phase insulin release in men. *Physiol Behav, 57*(6), 1089–1095.

Teff, K. L., Mattes, R. D., & Engelman, K. (1991). Cephalic phase insulin release in normal weight males: Verification and reliability. *Am J Physiol, 261*(4 Pt 1), E430–436. doi: 10.1152/ajpendo.1991.261.4.E430

Toller, S. V. (1999). Assessing the impact of anosmia: Review of a questionnaire's findings. *Chem Senses, 24*(6), 705–712.

Tomkins, S. S. (1962). *Affect, Imagery, Consciousness: Vol. 1. The Positive Affects.* New York: Springer.

Tordoff, M. G. (2001). Calcium: taste, intake, and appetite. *Physiol Rev, 81*(4), 1567–1597. doi:10.1152/physrev.2001.81.4.1567

Tsuda, M., & Aigaki, T. (2016). Evolution of sex-peptide in Drosophila. *Fly (Austin), 10*(4), 172–1777. doi:10.1080/19336934.2016.1193655

Twenge, J. M., Sherman, R. A., & Wells, B. E. (2017). Declines in sexual frequency among American adults, 1989–2014. *Arch Sex Behav, 46*(8), 2389–2401. doi:10.1007/s10508-017-0953-1

von Frisch, K., & Lindauer, M. (1956). The "language" and orientation of the honey bee. *Annual Review of Entomology, 1*, 45–58.

Von Skramlik, E. R. (1926). *Handbuch der physiologie der niederen sinne.* Leipzig: G. Thieme.

Wang, Z., & Wang, C. (2013). Is breath acetone a biomarker of diabetes? A historical review on breath acetone measurements. *J Breath Res, 7*(3), 037109. doi:10.1088/1752-7155/7/3/037109

Weber, S. T., & Heuberger, E. (2008). The impact of natural odors on affective states in humans. *Chem Senses, 33*(5), 441–447. doi:10.1093/chemse/bjn011

Wedekind, C., Seebeck, T., Bettens, F., & Paepke, A. J. (1995). MHC-dependent mate preferences in humans. *Proc Biol Sci, 260*(1359), 245–249. doi:10.1098/rspb.1995.0087

Welge-Lussen, A., Husner, A., Wolfensberger, M., & Hummel, T. (2009). Influence of simultaneous gustatory stimuli on orthonasal and retronasal olfaction. *Neurosci Lett, 454*(2), 124–128. doi:10.1016/j.neulet.2009.03.002

Wlodarski, R., & Dunbar, R. I. (2013). Examining the possible functions of kissing in romantic relationships. *Arch Sex Behav, 42*(8), 1415–1423. doi:10.1007/s10508-013-0190-1

Wlodarski, R., & Dunbar, R. I. (2014). What's in a kiss? The effect of romantic kissing on mating desirability. *Evol Psychol, 12*(1), 178–199.

Wolfe, J. M., Alvarez, G. A., Rosenholtz, R., Kuzmova, Y. I., & Sherman, A. M. (2011). Visual search for arbitrary objects in real scenes. *Atten Percept Psychophys, 73*(6), 1650–1671. doi:10.3758/s13414-011-0153-3

Wrangham, R. (2009). *Catching Fire: How Cooking Made Us Human.* New York: Basic Books.

Wysocki, C. J., Beauchamp, G. K., Reidinger, R. R., & Wellington, J. L. (1985). Access of large and nonvolatile molecules to the vomeronasal organ of mammals during social and feeding behaviors. *J Chem Ecol, 11*(9), 1147–1159. doi:10.1007/BF01024105

Wysocki, C. J., & Gilbert, A. N. (1989). National Geographic Smell Survey: Effects of age are heterogenous. *Ann N Y Acad Sci, 561*, 12–28.

Wysocki, C. J., Wellington, J. L., & Beauchamp, G. K. (1980). Access of urinary nonvolatiles to the mammalian vomeronasal organ. *Science, 207*(4432), 781–783.

Yamaguchi, S., & Ninomiya, K. (2000). Umami and food palatability.*J Nutr, 130*(4S Suppl), 921S–926S. doi:10.1093/jn/130.4.921S

Zelano, C., Bensafi, M., Porter, J., Mainland, J., Johnson, B., Bremner, E., . . . Sobel, N. (2005). Attentional modulation in human primary olfactory cortex. *Nat Neurosci, 8*(1), 114–120. doi:10.1038/nn1368

Zhao, H., Yang, J. R., Xu, H., & Zhang, J. (2010). Pseudogenization of the umami taste receptor gene Tas1r1 in the giant panda coincided with its dietary switch to bamboo. *Mol Biol Evol, 27*(12), 2669–2673. doi:10.1093/molbev/msq153

Zhong, S., Pinto, J. M., Wroblewski, K. E., & McClintock, M. K. (2018). Sensory dysfunction and sexuality in the U.S. population of older adults. *J Sex Med, 15*(4), 502–509. doi:10.1016/j.jsxm.2018.01.021

Zucco, G. M., Priftis, K., & Stevenson, R. J. (2015). From blindsight to blindsmell: A mini review. *Transl Neurosci, 6*(1), 8–12. doi:10.1515/tnsci-2015-0002

Acknowledgments

Foremost, I wish to thank Dr. Tyler Lorig who coparented this Element with me via a lengthy series of conversations on the topics included. This Element is not merely a traditional compendium and genuflection to the known understandings of the field, our "dogma," but also includes novel hypotheses and suppositions/speculations to encourage readers to stretch their understanding, consider the hypotheses offered, and possibly even test them. Additionally, I wish to thank Dr. Jim Enns for excellent editing and three anonymous reviewers for their helpful suggestions. The author was supported by a USDA/NIFA Hatch Grant via The New Jersey Agriculture and Experimental Station, Project No. NJ14120.

Perception

James T. Enns
The University of British Columbia

Editor James T. Enns is Professor at the University of British Columbia, where he researches the interaction of perception, attention, emotion, and social factors. He has previously been Editor of the *Journal of Experimental Psychology: Human Perception and Performance* and an Associate Editor at *Psychological Science, Consciousness and Cognition, Attention Perception & Psychophysics*, and *Visual Cognition*.

About the Series
The modern study of human perception includes event perception, bidirectional influences between perception and action, music, language, the integration of the senses, human action observation, and the important roles of emotion, motivation, and social factors. Each Element in the series combines authoritative literature reviews of foundational topics with forward-looking presentations of the recent developments on a given topic.

Cambridge Elements ≡

Perception

Elements in the Series

CPSIA information can be obtained
at www.ICGtesting.com
Printed in the USA
LVHW021133220719
624835LV00007B/150/P